Commun

Communities

*Stories of Christian
communities in Europe*

Text by Jeanne Hinton

Photographs by Christopher Phillips

eagle

Guildford, Surrey

British Library Cataloguing-in Publication Data. A catalogue record for this book is available from the British Library

Published by Eagle, an imprint of Inter Publishing Service (IPS) Ltd, 59 Woodbridge Road, Guildford, Surrey GU1 4RF

Lines from *Little Gidding* by T S Eliot reprinted by permission of Faber & Faber Ltd. Extracts taken from *St Francis at Prayer* edited by Wolfgang Bader and *Community and Growth* by Jean Vanier published and copyright 1988 and 1979 by Darton, Longman & Todd, used by permission of the publishers. *When the Lights Are On* from Iona Community Worship Book by permission of the Iona Community. *The Pollen of Peace* by permission of Roger Courtney. We also acknowledge permission from the communities in this book to reprint other material included.

All photographs used throughout the book Copyright © Christopher Phillips.

Typeset by The Electronic Book Factory Ltd, Fife, Scotland
Printed in Czech Republic
ISBN No: 0 86347 070 X

To all those pioneers of community mentioned in these pages, and to all those yet to come.

Contents

Introduction

WHEN I was asked if I would be interested to visit twelve communities in Europe to gather their stories for this book, I was delighted. The request was timely. It came as I was taking 'time out' from community life, and wanting to re-evaluate its contribution to my own life and to that of Church and society. My own experience of living in community began when I spent a year at Lee Abbey over thirty years ago, and more recently I have been a member for fifteen years of the Post Green Community.

My task in visiting these twelve communities during 1988 and 1989 was not to probe and analyse; it was to listen to their stories and to absorb what I could of the quality of each community's life. That is what Chris Phillips in pictures and I in words have to share with you. What we share is of a moment in time in the life of each community. By the time you come to read these stories some changes will have taken place. In community, life is never static; there is always change. My hope is that reading these stories will give you the desire to spend some time yourself visiting one or more such communities and learning from them what they have to share with you about living life.

Learning in everyday practical ways what life together is all about, and how to use the resources that God has given to help us to live lives that have meaning, is a large part of what these stories have to share with us. Included are stories of people of all ages who have found in visits to or membership of these communities a place where their search for friendship and relationship has been met. Friendship with God and with people; both are important, valued and nurtured. The 'how tos' vary. That is one of the delights. Each community is very definitely unique!

Learning to live fully is a continuing process of change and growth. 'Where else would I find a place where I can give myself so completely to my sisters and brothers, and where change is possible?' a member of one community comments. Here are people who are concerned about a quality of life for others as well as for themselves, and who are open themselves to change in order to help bring about this change in Church and society. What motivates them is the example of Jesus himself and the encouragement that the Bible gives that it is possible for people to live together justly and peaceably.

In these communities present living and future possibility have roots that are deep in the past. They draw inspiration and strength from generations of Christians who have walked this way before and made their contributions to the new society on earth – the 'new creation' – that God calls us to help in building. To hear the stories of these communities is to be introduced to a great number of women and men whose stories themselves enrich and inspire and who have a proven wisdom to share with us today that is invaluable for us.

Community life is not easy; it is fraught with difficulties. A little of this shows in the stories told in this book. Communities are fragile, vulnerable. Numbers of small communities start and exist only for a short while. Often the endings are painful to all concerned. But there have been and always will be communities. The longing to find ways of living together that work for all is a very strong desire. Those attempts of living in community that have seemingly failed are also part of this search.

The stories in this book are of only twelve of the many Christian communities that there are in Western Europe today. You will find at least one close to where you live if you ask. There are innumerable communities of this kind all over the Westernised world, recalling us to the art of living that a highly industrialised, technological society threatens. The communities exist not just for themselves, but for the sake of all of us. They are a resource for living. One way of drawing from this resource is to become if not a full member, then an associate or friend. Nearly all the communities in this book have a form of associate membership. I myself am still a friend of Lee Abbey, and have recently also become a companion of the Post Green Community, which commits me to support the community and to live under an adapted rule of life.

To become an associate or friend you will first need to make an initial visit and then spend time finding out more about a community: what you can give to it, what it can give to you. I hope this is the step that some of you will take when you have read this book.

Jeanne Hinton

Chapter One

Lee Abbey

I CAN never travel through the Valley of the Rocks on the North Devon coast in the south-west of England without remembering the first time I drove through the valley. Or rather was driven. I was eighteen years old, and was coming to join the Lee Abbey Community for a year. It was in November and through the late afternoon dusk I could just make out the outline of the weirdly-shaped rock formations through which we passed. I wondered where on earth I was coming to, and shivered with the strangeness of it all. I knew little of Lee Abbey, nothing of community life, and had never lived away from home before. The sombre eeriness of the rocks looming either side of the road and the gathering darkness did little to comfort me. I need not have worried; a year later it was only with great reluctance that I dragged myself away, back to what we called 'ordinary life'.

My first morning, I woke, looked out of the window, and gasped with delight. Even with the trees stripped bare and the sky overcast, Lee Abbey is incredibly beautiful. The wooded hillsides slope down to a small bay enclosed by high sea cliffs, and framing it all an old gnarled cedar tree. The tree is cut down now, and in summer

ice-cream vans and other tourist additions invade the Valley of the Rocks, but nothing can really alter the amazing beauty of the North Devon coast or of Lee Abbey itself. The Lee Abbey estate embraces 260 acres of wooded hillside and pasture-land, and the additions that have been made here over the years fit naturally into the setting. Indeed, Heritage and Civic Trust awards have been received for these developments.

Pioneering Spirit

D ESPITE its name, Lee Abbey is not an abbey as such, although it stands on old abbey lands. The original Ley Manor that stood here once is mentioned in the Domesday Book; *much* of the present house was rebuilt in the 1820s by a Squire Bailey. Its present history as a Christian community and as a holiday and conference centre began casually in 1934 when an Anglican priest, Roger de Pemberton, rented it for the summer holidays as a place to hold holiday house-parties. For some years before that Roger de Pemberton had been renting such places in different parts of the country to provide holiday house-parties during the summer vacation, mostly for young people. The idea behind these house-parties was to bring young people together for a holiday and also to explore what the Christian faith had to offer them.

These house-parties were soon to be interrupted by the outbreak of World War II. There was a short lapse and then Roger de Pemberton began again, but on a different basis. He now saw a need to provide a place where war workers could come for a rest and a change, and so his house-parties were extended to include adults as well as young people. They met a real need, for the war had shaken people's security, and sharpened questions about the Christian faith and the shaping of post-war society.

Roger de Pemberton was at that time vicar of a church in Rochester, Kent. A colleague was a layman, Leslie Sutton, who had worked for a time with the Worldwide Evangelisation Crusade in West Africa. Leslie, like Roger de Pemberton, had a deep desire to see a revitalised Church that had answers to the questions people were asking, and that faced them with what real commitment to Jesus Christ meant. Together they began to pray about finding a place where such house-parties could be run on a more permanent basis, a place that could be used under God to help revitalise the Church; in particular, the Church of England.

Soon they were joined by a third person. This was Jack Winslow, an Anglican clergyman; a High Churchman, whereas both Roger and Leslie were of a more evangelical persuasion. Jack Winslow had spent part of his life in India, and had founded a Christian

ashram, a community where Indians and Europeans lived and worked together on an equal basis. Mahatma Gandhi was a friend and a profound influence on him, as was an Indian Christian leader, Sundar Singh. He was to return to England in 1934 convinced that Indian spirituality and insights had a great deal to offer to the Western Church and world. Also before he left India he was to experience a mini-revival of his own. He came in touch with 'the Oxford Group' (a movement that emphasised listening prayerfully to God to receive practical and concrete guidance for action) founded by Frank Buchmann, and this led him to make a deeper dedication of his life to Christ. Back in England he began to work closely with the Oxford Group, although he was to distance himself from this movement when its direction changed and it became known under a new name, Moral Re-Armament. But these experiences had shown him not only his own need for a deeper commitment, but of the need of the Church for renewal.

In 1944 Jack Winslow went at Roger de Pemberton's invitation to help run a house-party which that summer was being held at Lee Abbey, at that time being used during the school terms as the wartime premises for a boys' preparatory school. Before he went Roger had told him that Lee Abbey might be the place they were looking for. That summer confirmed them in this view, and moves were made before the war ended to purchase the property. By now others shared their vision, and a body of trustees was appointed, a trust deed drawn up, and the following year, 1945, the war over, the property was bought. It was a venture of faith; £28,000 was the price, and more than that needed to do necessary repairs to the house and to furnish it. A legacy of £6,000 that Roger de Pemberton unexpectedly received secured the mortgage. The money to pay it off came in over the next years, mainly through people's gifts.

Roger de Pemberton became Lee Abbey's first warden, Leslie Sutton, its sub-warden, and Jack Winslow, the chaplain. In 1950, Geoffrey Rogers succeeded Roger de Pemberton as warden, and he, his wife Dora, and family stayed for fifteen years. The Rogers, Leslie and Phyllis Sutton and Jack Winslow, with others, formed a core team that laid the foundations of the present community and of Lee Abbey as a centre for evangelism within the Church of England. The time I spent at Lee Abbey as a member of the community was during this period, 1953–4. An early addition to the programme of house-parties was a youth camp held in August on the field just above Lee Bay. Many of my summer holidays during the late 'fifties and early 'sixties were spent helping to run these camps. It was a time for me of growing in faith, and for many of the young people who came the place where God first became real to them.

Places of Obedience

'INEVITABLY these beginnings had a pioneering spirit about them,' said John Perry, the warden until 1989. 'There was not the affluence that there is around today. Post-war it was a matter of rationing and making-do. That was the situation that Lee Abbey was raised up by God to respond to. What we've had to work at here over these past years is to understand what God wants of us today in a different situation.' It needs to help people 'see something of the costliness of commitment'. He saw the danger today of the Church selling 'a soft-line Christianity'. Dietrich Bonhoeffer's *Life Together* was, he said, required reading for community members.

> When Christ calls a man, he bids him come and die. It may be a death like that of the first disciples who had to leave home and work to follow him, or it may be a death like Luther's, who had to leave the monastery and go out into the world. But it is the same death every time . . . But how is a disciple to know what kind of cross is meant for him? He will find out as soon as he begins to follow his Lord and share his life. (Dietrich Bonhoeffer)

I have continued to return to Lee Abbey over the years, and have noticed changes that have taken place. The biggest change, of course, is that as the years have passed I have known fewer of the community, and then that the house itself has been made more comfortable. Now when I walk along the carpeted corridors I smile and remember that at one time there were no carpets, and as a 'house bod' one of my jobs was laboriously to dust and polish these floors. What impresses me, however, is that the spirit of the

place – the *feel* of it – remains the same. Places like Lee Abbey that are prayed and lived in over a period of time have this quality; they become 'special' or 'holy' places. I think this is one of the main reasons that I still feel as if I am coming home each time I return, and that so much that is past is still present to others in the same way.

Lee Abbey

Happy my lot cast in so fair a ground,
Where Exmoor flings down to the Devon seas
Her buttress hillsides thick with windswept trees,
And giant cliffs stand sentinel around.

But happier still that, mid such wealth outpoured,
Men's hearts are glad, and worship blends with mirth,
And new-found fellowship brings heav'n to earth,
And Christ Himself seems seated at our board.

So once again life's water turns to wine,
Ears deaf to Heaven's music are unsealed,
Blind eyes are opened to the light divine,
And minds possessed by demon fears are healed,
And men who cleave the wood and turn the sod
Stand, in rapt wonder, face to face with God.

Jack Winslow

One of the changes has been to develop a new kind of autumn/ spring programme, October to May. Traditionally this had been a time when Lee Abbey was either closed or had fewer guests. Now it is a period 'carefully geared into conferences, retreats, parish groups ... trying to discern where the Church and society is at ...' Autumn 88/spring 89 included a consultation on urban priority areas, a celebration of singleness, a creative arts weekend, a marriage refreshment course and a rural ministries conference. These not only met a need for those who came as guests, John said, but served an important function in raising issues for the community, too.

This desire to keep Christian commitment current with changing needs in society, has led Lee Abbey to extend itself outside Devon. In 1961 Lee Abbey called a Chapter of Friends to reflect and pray together about its future. The outcome was the decision to start a new work in London (Lee Abbey 2), a response to the need at that time for accommodation for overseas students. In 1964

the Lee Abbey International Students' Club was born, like Lee Abbey, Lynton, run by a resident community, but much smaller than the Devon community, with close links maintained between both. A more recent 'place of obedience', as John calls it, is the beginning of a third Lee Abbey. This is a response to the needs of Britain's inner cities and urban priority areas – a vision of a number of small communities established in partnership with local churches and other groups in inner-city areas. The first small community, the Aston Cottage Community, has just begun its life in Aston, Birmingham, amid overcrowded tightly terraced houses, a situation far removed indeed from rural Devon. The community is there to serve the local church in prayer and social action, to learn from local Christians and to live under a simple rule of life, in fellowship with the wider Lee Abbey Fellowship.

It was not possible for Chris and me to include Lee Abbey 2 and 3 as well as 1 in our schedule; each has its own separate stories.

Chris and I visited Lee Abbey in September, during a holiday week. The week had been designed for younger adults in response to frequent requests that Lee Abbey provide a week when there would be extra opportunities for outdoor activities. In fact, most of those who had booked in for the week were the not-so-young, but for those who were energetic enough there were abseiling, pony-trekking, gliding and orienteering, as well as the usual afternoon walks to places roundabout. For the not-so-energetic there was the possibility of a boat trip around the coast, or of brass rubbing in near-by Lynton.

It is usual for each holiday week to have a theme which is explored in the epilogue which ends each day. That week it was 'Attractive Attitudes'. Often there is also a guest speaker; for this week an Anglican clergyman from Torquay, Peter Larkin. Midweek Peter spoke about peace: being at peace with God, our neighbour and ourselves. He spoke of his own struggle to find such a peace, of the assumption that he had carried with him from his childhood that God was against him, and the relief that came when he realised that God was for him, not against him. This realisation had helped him to find not only peace with God, but also with himself and with others. These words struck a deep chord with several who listened, as we were to learn later in the week.

Lee Abbey can accommodate 125 guests. There are excellent facilities for families with small children; the private beach is safe for swimming and there are two tennis courts, a putting-green and a small sports hall where table-tennis, volley-ball and badminton can be played. Charges vary, depending on the season and there is a fund available to help those who may not be able to afford the full fee. Many return again and again. Indeed, there have been times when Lee Abbey has had to give preference to newcomers to keep the balance. The first evening at supper I sat next to a couple who had met each other at Lee Abbey thirty years before, and whose daughter was now a member of the community. 'We keep coming back,' they told me. Across the table, John, a young man in his thirties, looked a bit apprehensive. He had not been before, and had booked in with a friend who had cancelled. He had been uncertain whether to come alone. 'I've only been Christian four years,' he confided. 'I'm not sure what I'm in for here.'

After supper that evening there were interest groups. We could choose drama, singing, pebble painting, photography, making paper flowers, listening to contemporary music or a tour of the farm. I chose the tour of the farm. The young man who showed us round spoke knowledgeably of various cows. There were twenty-seven in all, and a number of calves. 'Can you actually tell one from another?' a small boy asked, awed. 'Oh, yes,' came the reply. The cows we learnt were all named after women who either were or had been members of the community: Rebecca, Suby, Gay, Margo, Loganberry. 'Loganberry!' 'Well, it was more of a nickname,' we were assured. I remembered that there had been a number of nicknames around when I was a member, too, usually to distinguish one Susan or Jane from another. But it had not been a custom then to name the cows after us!

Discipline of Service

TO MANAGE a farm, a 260-acre estate and to run a holiday house-party for 125 guests requires a large workforce. At the height of the summer holiday season the community usually numbers about eighty, with about seventy members at other times. The majority are single adults in their twenties and most come for one or two years. There are older members, but these are in the minority, as are the seven families that help make up the community. Some of the older members may stay longer, on an average up to five years. In the past there were those who stayed considerably longer than this and there was more of a mix of older and younger members. One of the present members said she felt to have long-termers was particularly important in the earlier years when the community was establishing itself. There are two members who have been at Lee Abbey for many years, and have now retired: Edna Madgwick and Audrey Copping. Now they live just off Lee Bay in a cottage that has been divided into two, and join in the community's life as much or as little as they wish.

The change in the make-up of the community is mostly due to changes in society. Now it is not so easy for teachers or nurses or those in other professions to take two years or more out and then return to professional life. The exceptions are likely to be those who have a particular skill that is needed, and also sense that God is calling them to join the community. Like Graham and Marion.

Graham and Marion came for a holiday with their family. At that time Graham had a job as a marketing manager. He recalled for us that one day during the holiday he had been looking at the view out of their bedroom window and had distinctly felt that God was saying to him, 'I want you here'. As they were leaving after the holiday, Debbie, their daughter, said, 'Mummy, why don't you and Daddy apply to join the community?' A coincidence indeed, but they waited a month before telephoning John Perry, then warden, to tell him that they were thinking of applying to join. John was surprised in his turn, for as he said to Graham, 'We've only been talking today about our need to find someone with professional marketing skills.'

John Perry and his wife, Gay,[1] have been at Lee Abbey nearly twelve years. There are others, both ordained and lay people, who help to make up the team that is responsible pastorally for both community and guests. For all seventy members of the community the work is demanding, and this, as John Perry explained, inevitably sets the tone of the community.

'. . . the pace of life, the constant change of guests, means that

Community Promises

Do you affirm before the Community your personal faith in Christ and your desire through prayer, study and service to seek a deep and mature faith?

I do

Do you understand by this that your mind, your time, your talents, your possessions and all your relationships are to be increasingly surrendered to Christ as Lord?

I do

Do you promise to be loyal to the Community in its aims, its work, its standards of behaviour and its disciplines?

I do

Are you prepared to learn to live in fellowship, being open to be known for what we are, accepting one another in Christ, and saying of others nothing that could not be said to them personally if love and wisdom required it?

I am

Have you accepted the discipline of regular private recollection through Bible reading and daily prayer?

I have

Do you intend to make the weekly Corporate Communion (or in the case of wives, the Sunday Communion Service) the central act of your work and worship?

I do

Are you ready to serve, in every way, those who come to us, seeking to help one another to a clearer and deeper knowledge of Christ, through your work and by your words?

I am

the community has got to be *on top* . . .' Dangerous words, as John quickly admitted, 'because we are all human, and in a community of seventy people, there are always going to be times when some need a bit of tender, loving care . . .' But the community was there to serve the guests. That community members did grow and find healing and wholeness happened, but that could not be their primary reason for joining. Some care therefore is taken in the selection of community members. For those who are accepted, it is just this demand and the discipline required of them that is valued, perhaps more in retrospect

---

[1] They left shortly after our visit, prior to John's consecration as Bishop of Southampton.

than at the time. I, too, can remember stammering my way through a farewell speech at the end of my year. 'This has without a doubt been the hardest year of my life so far, but I wouldn't have missed it for the world.' I heard an echo in twenty-year-old Jo's words to me, '. . . it hasn't always been easy, but I've loved every minute of it.'

For the community the day begins at 7.30 a.m. with breakfast, the one meal which the community eats apart from the guests. Before that, however, it is part of the community's rule of life that each member spends some time in personal prayer and Bible reading. That means an early rising; earlier still for those who have work to do on the farm or in the kitchen before breakfast. Breakfast over, the community gathers in the chapel for thirty minutes of corporate prayer. Attendance is obligatory; an essential spiritual discipline that undergirds the community's life and work. 'Indeed, anyone who misses prayers has to come and see me and tell me why,' John told us. Once a week prayers take the form of a Communion service. This service is also an opportunity to put right any differences that may have arisen; to say sorry if that is needed. The rule of life states that a member will not say anything about another behind his back that he or she would not lovingly say to him in person. 'In community if you fall out with someone you can't avoid them; you need to get it sorted out,' said Jo. Hard though she found it, she preferred this discipline to some of the bitchiness she had experienced outside of it. She and a friend had helped each other struggle through the hard times of living in community; for Jo the most difficult thing, 'learning to be open with my friends, to trust them with myself'.

Immediately community prayers are over, it is time for the guests' breakfast, and the hard work of the day has really begun. In earlier days guests helped with the washing-up after meals. Some of my own family remember this; always if there is a lot of washing-up to do after a meal, it is called a Lee Abbey wash-up! But this has changed; now there is a modernised kitchen, and there are machines to help do the work. The community's day is interspersed with times of relaxation and of prayer. Twice during the workday a loud bell rings and the community gathers; the first for mid-morning coffee, the second for afternoon tea. Again these are times when the community is apart from the guests; lunch and supper everyone eats together. Then there are departmental prayers, in the morning for those who work outside, in the afternoon, for those inside.

Chris and I were invited to join in these times with the community. 'Just turn up,' we were told. At noon we turned up for the estate team's departmental prayers, but it happened that we had chosen a day when instead of prayer it was a farewell lunch for Ian who was leaving that week. We all squeezed into the estate van and a car and drove along the winding cliff road to a near-by pub. Over lunch I talked with Rob, who said he also would be leaving the

community soon. He was sorry, he would miss it. He had not long been a Christian, and had known when he became one that he would need the close support of others in learning how to live as a Christian. He had not found this close support in any church he had attended. Now after two years as a member of the Lee Abbey Community, he felt it would be good to put into practice in ordinary life what he had learnt. But he was even more convinced than he had been before that close support was essential to living an effective Christian life; he thought he might become a Third Order Franciscan.

The day-to-day running of Lee Abbey is managed by its Chapter, which includes chaplains and departmental leaders, and other longer serving and older members. John Perry told us that he had made a point during his time as warden to move the community towards as much shared responsibility as possible. This had included 'up-grading' the positions of heads of teams: estate, household, kitchen and office. Decisions about matters affecting them are also shared within these teams. For many of the younger members of the community this gives them perhaps their first opportunity to be responsible for others and for real decision-making. Jo had been

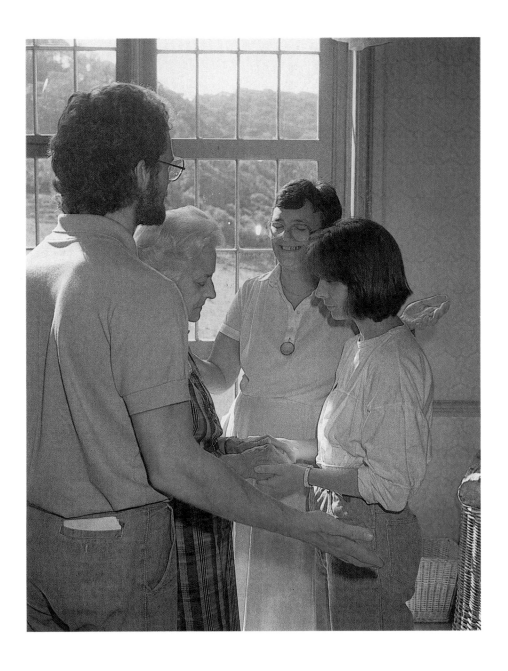

head of the house team for a year; a major responsibility, which had helped her to discover gifts she didn't know she had.

Another way in which members discover gifts they didn't know they had is through creativity: writing, composing, acting, singing. While we were there the community performed a gospel musical, *The Kingdom, the Power and the Glory*, written, composed and performed by members, and nearly all took part.

'Everyone is creative,' said Alan, one of the chaplains and also one of the team of three responsible for the musical. 'Everybody's got a gift, and developing that gift has to do not just with the gift itself, but with personal maturity.' For him one of the greatest privileges of being a chaplain at Lee Abbey was seeing 'some people come in who are essentially adolescents, going out confident adults'.

Community members receive a pocket-money allowance, plus board, the allowance slightly more for longer-term members and those with families. Members come from all over the world, in recent years from Germany, Holland, Hungary, South Africa, Kenya and New Zealand.

In such a large and busy community it is essential that some time is found for members to be together socially. Everyone is part of a family or home group which meets weekly. Chris and I were invited to one at Graham's and Marion's home. Again it was a farewell party; at the close of the season, there are a lot of farewells. Susan was leaving to return to America, and there were stars and stripes and carrot cake as well as home-made wine and coffee. Conversation was mostly about people's departures, and do you remember when . . . ?

A lot of experience is packed into two to five years, and leaving is always a wrench. This is recognised and a tradition has grown up to help in the actual departure. We left before Ian's departure, but we were told that when the time came the bell would ring and all the community would gather in the yard. A large circle would be formed and Ian would move around the circle, saying his goodbyes. In this way no one is missed out, but more importantly the whole community is gathered to mark this as an important transition in Ian's life and to support him in it. Before that Ian would have made his leaving speech to the community at a meeting nearest to his departure, been given a book signed by all fellow-members, and been prayed for by the community at prayers that same morning. We did not have a leaving circle when I left, but I still have my book, signed by all my fellow-members; a treasured possession. Geoffrey and Dora's names are there, and Leslie and Phyllis Sutton's, and Jack's, Edna Madgwick's too.

'Vulnerable Making'

'ALL THAT STUFF that Bonhoeffer talked about, that it is only when you become disillusioned about community, that you really begin to live in it, is so true.' In his five years as chaplain Alan Smith had seen a number of community members come and go. In his experience it was those who were fearful about coming or even reluctant, who had the easier time. Those who imagined they were coming to a 'bed of roses', as Jo told me she did, inevitably found it hard. He had thought it was going to be awful, but hadn't found it so difficult. Nevertheless, it had been 'very vulnerable making'. For him too, it was because 'you can't avoid people. In a parish if you have a hard day you just don't go to visit anybody or you only visit the safe people, but here you can't do that. If you're feeling snappy, everyone knows you're feeling snappy.'

When Lee Abbey takes teams to conduct missions in churches around the country, part of the message it takes is that all Christians are called to a commitment to each other as an integral part of the Christian life. John Perry saw this as increasingly important in today's society. 'We are saying something about style of life, about the people of God knowing their interdependence.' Lee Abbey is increasing the number of missions it runs each year, and including in its mission teams Lee Abbey friends, who are able to share from experience what it means to work out in a different situation what they have learnt from the Lee Abbey Community.

At the Communion service which marked the ending of the holiday week, a young man got to his feet and with difficulty said that during the week he had cried for the first time in his life. It had been such a release; he knew that God had touched him and healed a deep wound in his life. He was in tears as he said it. It was the time during the service when guests are invited to share what God has done for them during the week. After this young man spoke, there was a long silence. This was broken eventually by a much older man heaving himself to his feet. He had, he said, been challenged deeply by what Peter Larkin had said earlier in the week about being at peace with God, himself and others. His difficulty was how to find peace with himself. He had gone to the chapel to pray, and to his amazement had begun to cry. He had gone on crying for several hours. He had not cried like that since he was a child; he felt a new person.

As these two men spoke, my mind was on an incident that had happened at the house team's departmental prayers the afternoon I had been present. These had taken place with all of us sitting on the floor of the chapel, and there had been discussion about a Bible passage, and a time of prayer. A song had been sung, and during it a young woman had suddenly burst into tears. No one made any to-do about it, but there was an emphatic silence as she said that her grandmother had died the night before, and . . . An arm was put around her, a prayer said. 'Sorry,' said Polly to the others, brushing away her tears. But no one minded; this was a moment for some tender, loving care.

When the Communion service was over, I went for a walk. As I climbed to the tower overlooking Lee Bay, I thought about the week. What is it, I thought, about society that demands of men in particular that they cut off all feeling; that says it is unmanly to cry? And how is it, I thought, that we live in a society that educates young people for work, but does so little to prepare them for life? That leaves many still adolescents at age twenty or more. Looking back, I included myself in this. Then I thought of all I have learnt in community about living with others, with myself and with God and said thank you for it.

The holiday week ended, it was time for us guests to depart. There is a tradition, too, to guests' departures from Lee Abbey. Thirty years back the big bell was rung and all the community gathered under the archway to say their goodbyes. Then the coaches would come, perhaps three or four, to take the departing guests to Barnstaple station where they would catch trains to wherever. There were not so many cars then. It took a long time to fill all the coaches; eventually they would leave and we would trail back to the house to our various tasks. We were always sad to see people go, but never sure we were up to welcoming further coachloads later that same day, and being as John says 'on top'. It *was* hard work.

The big bell still chimes; not all the community come now to say goodbye, but all those who have been part of the host team for that week do. People gather not under the archway at the entrance where the coaches used to turn, but in the courtyard. Here by the reception office, luggage is loaded into cars.

'But, it's not really real, is it?' John, whom I had met at supper on our first evening, stood beside me. There was a wistful sound to his voice as he made his comment. He was voicing what many have voiced over the years. Is such a life possible back in the 'real world'? John said he was not convinced that it was possible. He moved away. He had people to say goodbye to; so had I. Eventually Chris and I got into Chris's car and left. As we did so, I looked back. John was still standing there by his car, reluctant to leave.

CHAPTER TWO

Little Gidding

A N ELDERLY woman living in a Sussex village opened the *Guardian* one morning and read of a couple in Huntingdonshire who were starting a Christian community at a place called Little Gidding. Sixty-eight years old, she was nevertheless eager for some new adventure. Widowed at the age of fifty-one, she had subsequently had some experience of living as part of a religious community, and the couple she read about were asking for others to come and join them. She wrote, visited, and decided to do so. Two years later the couple she had joined moved on elsewhere. That might have been the end of that. But it was not the end. It was a new beginning.

There had been a community at Little Gidding in the seventeenth century. It had attracted the attention of Charles I – with disastrous consequences as it turned out. In 1936 T. S. Eliot made a pilgrimage to Little Gidding and wrote a poem about the place and the community which made its name known to many who had never heard of it. He also helped to form the Friends of Little Gidding, a group of interested people who set about restoring Little Gidding church and established an annual pilgrimage to it.

When Veronica moved from her Sussex home, she was stepping into a bit of history rooted deep in English soil – and there is a lot of that at Little Gidding, particularly if you visit as Chris and I did in mid-winter, one of the wettest that I can remember. The countryside in that area on the borders of the Fens can be as bleak as it is also beautiful; somewhat different from the charm of rural Sussex and 'an old Elizabethan house up a bridle path, with moorhens on the pond in the garden', as Veronica described her previous home to us. But in moving from there to Little Gidding she was helping to bring forth a new shoot from that original seventeenth-century root. Indeed, the present community has called itself the Community of Christ the Sower.

'How many are there of you now?' I asked Margaret, as she ladled out soup for the dozen or so people who gathered for lunch the day we visited.

'Well,' she said, 'I'll go round the courtyard first. That's the easiest way to count.

'There's Ann and Michael. Then there's Lawrence and Di who have three children including baby twins. Next to them is Veronica, followed by David and Liz and their two little girls. Chris and Pat

live in the next house which Chris converted from a two-storey barn. They have two children: Anna, who is eleven, and Jonathan, who is ten. Then there are Martin and Maureen and their little boy David. Martin is Warden of Little Gidding, and also has a job as a probation officer. In the main house Valerie and Ruth live in a flat on one side of the house, and I live in a flat on the opposite side . . .'

She then went on to tell me of those who are at Great Gidding, and those who live five miles away at Leighton Bromswold. I laughed, I had expected her to say ten or twenty or thirty people. It was in fact the perfect answer. Community is about people, and people mattering as individuals and to each other. It is not about numbers and statistics. That is one of its attractions.

The courtyard she mentioned was formerly part of the old farmyard, now an attractive semicircle of houses built in 1980, using old materials, including the timber frame of a barn that had been there in the seventeenth century. The ground floor of the main house consists of various community rooms and a 'parlour' where visitors can buy light refreshments, books and postcards. It is open from 11 a.m. to 5 p.m. from Monday to Saturday, and from 2 p.m. to 5 p.m. on Sundays. The parlour also contains a small exhibition telling the story of the community going back to the seventeenth century.

The Original Community

THE FOUNDER of the first Little Gidding community, Nicholas Ferrar, has been likened by his biographer, Alan Maycock, to Ferrar's contemporary, Oliver Cromwell. Indeed, Alan Maycock asserts that had Ferrar not withdrawn from public life he 'might have changed the course of history', and his name be as familiar to us as that of Cromwell. At least one member of the present community had learnt about Nicholas Ferrar at school, and that was one of the factors in her later joining the community. I, however, had not heard of his name until recently and then only through being a member of such a Christian community myself.

Born in 1592, within the sound of London's Bow Bells, into a prosperous family, Nicholas Ferrar was sent at the early age of eight to one of the newly formed boarding or public schools. At thirteen he moved from there to Clare College, Cambridge; the average age of university entrance was then fifteen or sixteen. Young as he was his wit and talent was such that within a year he had been elected a Fellow Commoner and was sitting at the High Table entertaining not only his fellow students, but masters as well.

It looked as though he was all set for a brilliant academic career. But his constitution was poor, and at the age of twenty-one he was advised by his doctor to leave Cambridge and travel abroad for his health. This was to have a profound effect on the subsequent course of Nicholas's life. Brought up in a deeply religious home, he had responded early to its influence. His favourite book was Foxe's *Book of Martyrs*, and he had decided he wanted to become a clergyman. Travel, however, changed his mind, for he responded to the challenge and excitement of what he saw and experienced. On his return he decided to follow in his father's footsteps and become a businessman. His father had helped to found the Virginia Company, with its interests in the expanding trade in the New World, and Nicholas now joined that company.

His travels in Europe also influenced him in other ways. He was impressed by what he saw of the Protestant Anabaptist communities (the radical 'left-wing' of the Reformation, including the Hutterites and Mennonites.) and their simplicity of life, and also by the spiritual fervour of the new Catholic religious orders that were then being founded. He was to remember them later on.

As a businessman he and the Virginia Company prospered. So much so that his company earned the hostility of others who saw their interests threatened. This was to lead to the company's being sued and eventually closed. Nicholas Ferrar led the company's defence himself to the point of successfully bringing about the impeachment of one of its major antagonists, the Earl of Middlesex, on charges of bribery and corruption. It was this success that proved

the catalyst for the next major change in Ferrar's life. He was a
deeply sensitive and religious man and he was by now disenchanted
with his way of life. It was at this point he decided to withdraw
from public life and to set about founding a Christian community
similar in some ways to those he had visited on the Continent, but
not so austere in its simplicity of life as those of the Anabaptists or
as extravagant in its piety as those of the new Catholic religious
orders. He wanted to found a community particularly suited to the
English temperament and people. He looked for a possible location
and found Little Gidding 'in the heart of the English countryside'.

It was while he was defending his company that Nicholas Ferrar
made a lifelong friend of the English poet, George Herbert. Each
was to influence the other, and both were ordained deacon in the
same year, 1626. George Herbert became an honorary canon of
Lincoln Cathedral, which carried with it the living of Leighton
Bromswold, only five miles from Little Gidding. George Herbert
never lived there. He was to spend most of the rest of his life
working as a country parson, as rector of Bemerton, near Salisbury, but he retained the living of Leighton Bromswold, and paid
for and supervised the restoration of the church there, parts
of which date back to before the thirteenth century. He and
Nicholas Ferrar remained in constant contact and, as a close
friend, adviser and supporter of Ferrar, George Herbert's name
crops up frequently in the ongoing development of the community
at Little Gidding.

Love

Love bade me welcome; yet my soul drew back,
   Guiltie of dust and sinne.
But quick-ey'd Love, observing me grow slack
   From my first entrance in,
Drew nearer to me, sweetly questioning,
   If I lack'd any thing.
A guest, I answer'd, worthy to be here:
   Love said, You shall be he.
I the unkinde, ungratefull? Ah my deare,
   I cannot look on thee.
Love took my hand, and smiling did reply,
   Who made the eyes but I?
Truth Lord, but I have marr'd them: let my shame
   Go where it doth deserve.
And know you not, sayes Love, who bore the blame?
   My deare, then I will serve.
You must sit down, sayes Love, and taste my meat:
   So I did sit and eat.

George Herbert (1593–1633)

When Nicholas Ferrar first visited Little Gidding all that he saw was a manor house in need of repair, a disused church used as a barn for storing hay, and a few shepherds' cottages. Although they were uninhabited and uninviting, he must have felt they suited his purposes well. Even today, while not uninviting it seems remote, even though it is only seventy miles from London and not far from the busy A1 trunk road. As a community it stands on its own; the nearest village Great Gidding is only two miles away, but cannot be seen from Little Gidding itself.

Not married himself, Nicholas Ferrar gathered around himself other members of the Ferrar family and these formed the basis of that first community: his widowed mother, Mary, his elder brother, John, and wife, Bathsheba, and their two children; his eldest sister, Susannah, and her husband, John Collett. Others joined them: three single men who became schoolmasters to the children and four elderly widows. Later the school established as part of the household was opened to other girls and boys from surrounding villages.

Nicholas Ferrar's aim in forming such a community was to be able to arrange ordinary family life in such a way that daily prayer was central to it. Three times a day the family walked from the house to the church to say first, Morning Prayer, then the Litany, and then Evening Prayer, all from the Book of Common Prayer. Each service

was followed by a family meal: breakfast, lunch, supper. Later the practice of a nightly vigil was added, with different members of the family staying up from nine o'clock to one o'clock at which time Nicholas woke from sleep and spent the rest of the night alone in prayer, reciting the Psalms. His desire was to develop a more contemplative form of prayer than the Prayer Book alone allowed.

In establishing the spiritual discipline of that community Ferrar was combining what he most liked of both Protestant and Catholic spirituality as he had met it on his earlier travels. In this the community was unique, for the seventeenth century was a time of intense religious squabbles over worship and ceremony; squabbles that had political implications, for England wanted to be free of Popish domination. It was a time when high churchmen held to and continued to love adornment and ceremony, while the Puritans abhorred all such as Popish idolatry. In the church at Little Gidding the Ferrars included a small organ, since they loved music, and the church was adorned with richly embroidered tapestries made by the women of the community. But their daily services and their lives were simple, although not austere. None of the members took vows for Nicholas Ferrar did not agree with this.

There were many visitors, so many that the community had to find some way of bringing order to this part of their lives. Strangers were made welcome, given a drink of wine or ale, their questions answered, and they were then sent away. The only exceptions to this rule were friends and acquaintances. One such exception was that the community gave hospitality to Catholic priests at a time when it was dangerous to do so. They did not stay at Little Gidding as this was considered too dangerous, but they stayed at nearby Leighton Bromswold, where the Duchess of Lennox, a friend of the community, hid them in her lodge, and from there they came to Little Gidding to spend time with Nicholas Ferrar. His desire was to help bring about a reconciliation between Catholics and Protestants.

He then comes to the King, saying, 'Sir, you shall, if you please to go with me, see another good thing, that will like you well.'

'What's that?' said the King.

'The curious lodgings in the alms-houses provided for four poor widows, by the old gentlewoman mother of the family.'

'What,' said the King, 'have you been there before me already? I meant to see them before I went.'

'Sir, I will lead you the way,' said the Palsgrave.

So the King and Prince followed him, and the Duke. So come into the widow's rooms, which were handsomely wainscotted, and four beds in them, after the Dutch manner of their alms-houses, all along the walls; the room being rubbed, and cleanly kept, the King looking well about him, and upon all things, said 'I will believe your

judgement another time . . . It's passing neat and well-kept, and of good example.'

'Sir,' said one, 'it resembles much the chapel, each being wainscotted and pillared and arched.'

'Truly this is worth the sight,' [said the King]. 'I did not think to have seen a thing in this kind, that so well pleaseth me. God's blessing be upon the founders of it! Time was,' speaking to the Palsgrave, 'that you would have thought such a lodging not amiss.'

'Yea, sir,' said he, 'and happy I had had it full often.'

So some questions the King asked about the widows &c. and
going out of the room into a long arbour in the garden, and looking
back behind him upon the company, said, 'We may not come into
a place we like so well, and see so much charity, and leave only
a verbal commendation. Where is Ferrar?' Who, being called, the
King, putting out his hand, said to my Lord Duke of Richmond,
'Lo, five pieces I give to be distributed by him unto several poor
people here about you, that they may pray for my speedy and
safe return again. It is all I have, else they should have more;'
(these he had won the night before of the Palsgrave at cards at
Huntingdon).

While the King was walking, and talking, and commending the
fine and pleasant situation of the house upon a little hill as it stood
upon, to divers around him, saying, 'Gidding is a happy place in
many respects; I am glad I have seen it;' the young lords had gone
into the buttery, and there found apple pies and cheese cakes &c.,
and came out with pieces in their hands into the parlour to the
Prince, and merrily said, 'Sir, will your highness taste; it is a good
apple pie as ever we eat.'

The Prince laughed heartily at them: so wine was brought.

The King came in, saying, 'It grows late; the sun is going down;
we must away.' So their horses were brought to the door. (*The King
at Little Gidding*, © Little Gidding Books, 1987.)

Early on, Nicholas Ferrar conceived the idea of putting together
a narrative of the life of Christ drawn from the gospels, read in
sequence with the parallel parts from each gospel side by side.
Copies of the gospels were cut up and pasted together, thus making
a single volume or concordance. It was this that first brought the
community to the attention of King Charles I. In the early 1630s
he was staying a few miles away, heard of this book, and sent a
messenger to ask if he could borrow it. He kept it for several months,
using it for his own devotions, and then asked the community to
make him his own copy.

In March 1642 the king visited Little Gidding. Married to a
Catholic wife, he was suspected of Catholic loyalties. His visit
was just prior to the outbreak of the Civil War, which was to end
with King Charles's defeat by the Protestant Cromwell and to his
being beheaded in 1649. After his defeat by the Parliamentarian
forces, the king returned to Little Gidding seeking refuge. Fearing
that he would not be safe there, John Ferrar hid him in a private
house some miles away. The king left the following morning and
was arrested soon afterwards. But the community paid dearly for
the friendship they had given him. It had already gained enemies
as well as friends, not least because it befriended Catholics and
was accused itself of Papist practices. Now having heard that the
king had taken refuge at Little Gidding, Cromwell sent his troops

to ransack the house and church. For safety's sake the family left, returning after a while and remaining another eleven years, but the church was left unadorned, for they did not want to incur further Puritan wrath.

Nicholas Ferrar had died in 1637 before these happenings. His brother John had taken over the leadership of the community. After John's death in 1657 the place reverted to a family home. But some three centuries later Ferrar's biographer, Alan Maycock, was still to experience Little Gidding as a holy place, and to pose the question, 'Will the torch ever be relighted in this holy place? Will it ever again belong to a community who will pass to and from the church in procession for the daily offices, following the "good old way" of devotion to the service of God and their fellowmen?'

Re-awakening Interest

HOLY PLACES have a way of living on, and of renewing themselves. Even if the buildings are a heap of ruins, or there are no ruins left, people visiting many centuries later may be struck by some strange sense of *something other*. This was certainly the poet T. S. Eliot's experience when he visited Little Gidding in 1936.

If you came this way,
Taking the route you would be likely to take
From the place you would be likely to come from,
If you came this way in May time, you would find the hedges
White again, in May, with voluptuary sweetness.
It would be the same at the end of the journey,
If you came at night like a broken king,
If you came by day not knowing what you came for,
It would be the same, when you leave the rough road
And turn behind the pigsty to the dull façade
And the tombstone. And what you thought you came for
Is only a shell, a husk of meaning
From which the purpose breaks only when it is fulfilled
If at all. Either you had no purpose
Or the purpose is beyond the end you figured
And is altered in fulfilment. There are other places
Which also are the world's end, some at the sea jaw
Or over a dark lake, in a desert or a city –
But this is the nearest, in place and time,
Now and in England.

If you came this way,
Taking any route, starting from anywhere,
At any time or at any season,
It would always be the same: you would have to put off
Sense and notion. You are not here to verify,
Instruct yourself, or inform curiosity
Or carry report. You are here to kneel
Where prayer has been made valid.

With Alan Maycock, Ferrar's biographer, T. S. Eliot re-awakened interest in the Little Gidding community at a time (mid-twentieth century) when there was a growing interest worldwide in the founding of such communities. The formation at that time of the Friends of Little Gidding led to one couple moving there with the intention of doing this, but their personal resources were depleted in the attempt and they left after three years. Which brings us back to Veronica Gray who 'did not want to move again'.

Little Gidding Today

VERONICA had been joined by another couple, Sarah and Robert Van de Weyer, and their two children, Sylvain and Aidan. That was in 1977. Robert is now pastor of the community which numbers thirty-eight full members, twenty-eight adults and ten children, and is also priest-in-charge of Great with Little and Steeple Gidding,

Hamerton, Winwick and Upton with Copingford. In this part of England there are many old churches too big for the present number of inhabitants. The combined population of all these parishes is less than seven hundred. Whole villages were wiped out in the Black Death of the mid-fourteenth century; all that survived were the big stone churches, solemn reminders of that tragic episode in English history.

Sarah and Robert met at university, and then spent some time in India, both seeking a spiritual faith and attracted at that time to Eastern religions. They lived for a period alongside a Christian ashram or community, and it was during their time in India that Robert decided that for six months he would try to live according to the teachings of Jesus, choosing him for his guru or religious teacher.

Before the end of this period he was a convinced Christian. Sarah grew more gradually into accepting the Christian faith as her own. By the time they returned to England they were both Christians, and interested in the possibility of living in a Christian community in England.

First they returned to the North of England where they had lived previously, for part of the time in a small miner's cottage near Durham. Now in Leighton Bromswold they live in a red-brick Jacobean manor, originally built in 1616 as a gatehouse and partly surrounded by a moat.

'Goodness, a moat!' I exclaimed when Chris and I arrived and stumbled our way up the muddy path towards the house. It was bitterly cold and raining and we had had difficulty finding our way. Most of the signposts had been turned round and were pointing the other way we discovered later. The Jacobean house we were expecting; the moat we were not. 'I giggle every time I turn the corner and see the house. To think I live here,' says Sarah. East Anglia is, however, full of such surprises, and this is one of the unexpected pleasures of walking or driving round this part of England.

As a child Robert had dreamt of living in a community, and later as a teenager he had been browsing through some books on a second-hand bookstall in London and came across the biography of Nicholas Ferrar. It fed his dream of some day belonging to such a community. That his and Sarah's return to England should have coincided with the uncertain beginnings of re-establishing a Community at Little Gidding is one coincidence; another is that when the Van de Weyers moved in 1986 from Little Gidding itself to form another arm of the community at Castle House, Leighton Bromswold, they discovered that Robert was related by blood to one of its previous owners, no other than Katherine Clifton, the Duchess of Lennox, who had befriended the community in the seventeenth century. A great grandfather of Robert had married one of her descendants. Ferrar's friend, George Herbert had held services in the parlour of Castle House during the restoration of the parish church in the 1600s. Now the same room is set aside as a chapel for the use of the community. To eat a meal at Castle House is to meet these venerable forebears for their portraits hang on the walls by the dining table.

'That's Nicholas Ferrar, that's Mary Ferrar, and that's ... George Herbert, and that's ... that's ... our ancestor ...', eleven-year-old Sylvain was to tell us at supper on our first evening.

In the Ferrars' time the community was very much an extended family household. Today any person wishing to join the community visits once or twice, talks with Robert as the pastor and gets to know some of the members. Then if it seems right to all concerned the new member is asked to make a commitment to stay for at least one year. At Little Gidding itself there might be a house available owned by the community. At Great Gidding or Leighton Bromswold where there are also community members, it would be a matter of buying or renting a house or other accommodation. Those who live in houses owned by the community have a choice of putting any capital from the sale of a previous home into a fund administered by the community and, on leaving, receiving a sum as near to its increased market value as possible. To put capital into the community's fund is not compulsory; the money can be invested elsewhere. Now, as in Nicholas Ferrar's time, no vows are taken. After a year full membership is considered. At this point the whole community is involved in the decision that is made. After this, membership is reviewed annually, but all of those to whom we talked presumed they would stay, probably permanently.

There is a simple rule of life: to pray together once a day, to celebrate Communion and if possible to share a meal with other community members at least once a week, to commit time and resources to God's service and to aim to live peaceably with God and others. The rule of life is made as easy as possible for ordinary Christians, some of whom will be earning a living outside the community and some of whom will be married and have family responsibilities. The words 'Those able to do so' and 'if possible' appear frequently in the simple rule. Not all can pray together every day or be at the weekly Eucharist. For those who can there are prayers each morning both at Little Gidding and at Leighton Bromswold; twice a week the Eucharist is celebrated. This is on Wednesday evening and Saturday – not Sunday, as members also belong to local churches of different denominations. The community does not see itself as an alternative church, but an addition to it.

The one aspect of the rule that is obligatory is the annual renewal of covenant made each autumn. New members are formally received at this time. There is also an annual review of stewardship of time and resources. This happens during the Christmas season. Each member talks with the pastor about the way she or he is balancing prayer, work and leisure, and about their stewardship of money and material resources. It is at this point each year that any adjustment may be made to members' giving to the community's own needs. An example given was that if there are fewer members living in housing available at Little Gidding some may need to pay higher rents. People pay what they can afford. The aim is to find a right balance between the claims of family, community, local church and the poor and deprived of the world.

Lent is also a time for review, but this time for reviewing relationships within and without the community. Each member is asked to reflect on whether he or she is at peace with God and with others. This may entail talking confidentially with a pastor. The period of reflection is followed by a service of reconciliation.

Reconciliation

Each year during Lent, and at other times if it seems necessary, we have a service of reconciliation. Beforehand we each find time for personal reflection, perhaps with the confidential counsel of a pastor, seeking to discern those aspects of our lives where we are not at peace with God and with other people.

This service takes place during Communion, after the Teaching section.

President   As God through the death and resurrection of his Son has reconciled mankind to himself, we pray that we may grow and mature in the image of the risen Christ.

People   **We seek to live in harmony with one another, bearing witness to the peace to which all people are called.**

President   God is infinitely patient in his desire for us to repent, that we in turn may be tolerant and compassionate.

People   **May we be slow to judge the sins of others and quick to confess our own, forgiving others as Christ forgives us.**

President   God in his mercy makes us whole, that we who are weak and foolish may proclaim his power and wisdom.

People   **May we always be ready to open our hearts to others, reaching out to all we meet with the hand of his love.**

The President and another person lay hands on those who wish to receive a sign of God's reconciling love. They begin by laying hands on one another. As the sign is made, the President may say, 'May Almighty God make you whole in body, mind and spirit, according to his will', and the person receiving the sign may say, 'Amen'. When all who wish have received the sign, the following words are spoken:

President   By the wounds of Christ we are made whole, that we may show forth his glory in the world.

People   **May we live in union with him, in all things giving thanks to God.**

A hymn may be sung.
(The Little Gidding Prayer Book)

The rule is no more nor less than that. The aim is to give each individual and family the freedom to develop life and faith as seems appropriate. In practice, it is not always easy to maintain this desired balance between allowing members the freedom to grow according to their own inclinations and desires, and maintaining a communal life that is satisfying to all. Inevitably there is a pendulum swing; regular review is necessary.

Some form of leadership is also necessary. As a preparation for joining Little Gidding, Sarah and Robert visited a number of monastic communities, including some in Ethiopia, dating back to the first desert communities of the second century. In Ethiopia they discovered that the monks had developed a form of leadership that was not strictly democratic, but not autocratic either. It worked by separating managerial and pastoral functions. This is the form of leadership adopted by Little Gidding. Different areas of the community's life are managed by particular individuals, who while accountable to the whole community are also free to make responsible decisions in their own areas. In practice again decisions are often taken by some form of consultation. There was a great deal of conversation at meals and at other times when we visited over the purchase of a new photocopier. The evening we left members were gathering together to talk more formally about this matter. With such matters in the hands of managers, pastors are then free to concern themselves with the more personal aspects of the community's life and of its members. This division of leadership functions guards against the kind of autocracy that can happen in communities where members' lives are managed for them by an excessive authoritarianism. When we visited there were several managers managing, but Robert was still the only pastor. This, however, was just about to change and the hope is that in time there will be several who are sharing the task.

Excess is what the community does not espouse in any form. Ordinariness, practicality, simplicity are words used. At Little Gidding and Leighton Bromswold the rooms that are used communally are clean, tidy and yet homely. The meals, too, were simple. While visiting we ate lentils and beans twice, meat once. Bread and soup and cheese for lunch, cereal and toast for breakfast. We drank apple juice at two meals, a glass of sherry before one!

The emphasis is on being together, rather than doing anything particular together. What is done communally is done either to meet a practical need or because one or more members have a particular interest they want to share. An example of the latter is that two couples with young families are interested in starting a small school; an example of meeting a practical need is the small farm that consists of five acres of land, one cow to milk, four cows to fatten, three or more pigs in the summer, one sheep, numbers of fruit bushes and trees and several allotments. Different members share the responsibilities here.

Another practical need is for more buildings. One member who has the necessary skills oversees these projects, doing much of the manual work himself. Others are occupied with young children, or managing the home or are in employment outside. One is working full-time in the parish, another is a probation officer; others a social worker, a banker, a solicitor, an economist, a telephone engineer, a teacher, an artist. Most therefore are in the middle to higher income brackets. The community is indeed rather middle-class, and in the words of one American guest 'very English'.

Renewal of English Spirituality

BY 'very English' was meant, we discovered, 'somewhat reticent, a bit private'. In many ways the present community is consciously so. Balance, moderation, tolerance are words that cropped up often in conversation about the community's life and aims, as did an individual's or family's need for privacy. Members of the community have also compiled and had published an anthology of English prose and poetry, *The English Spirit*, its aim to help put English Christians back in touch with their lost spiritual roots.

'There are two things really,' Robert explained to us, 'the one is best summed up in the words *homeliness*, and then there is the notion of formal or structured prayer being for everybody.

'We English are basically a practical lot. We are not into high-flown intellectual theories or spiritual ecstasy. We like to find our religion amid the pots and the pans.

'In the seventeenth century Ferrar and Herbert were seeking to interpret Cranmer's vision of liturgical prayer being for the whole church and for families. In this way the English Reformation steered a middle way between a Catholic tendency to see prayer as a specialist activity, and the tendency of other parts of the Protestant Reformation to adopt more spontaneous forms of prayer.'

Cranmer's Book of Common Prayer thus holds a special place within the life of Little Gidding Community, although not all its members are Anglican. And as in the seventeenth century the community compiled its book of Bible readings, so the present community has put together its Little Gidding prayer book, incorporating their simple rule of life. There are special sets of prayers or services for each part of the rule: daily prayer, communion, covenant, stewardship, reconciliation, ministry. 'It is daily prayer being lived out in daily life. The test is what happens at work or in the home,' one member told us.

This was the 'good old way' that before he died Nicholas Ferrar commended to his brother John.

'It is the right, good, old way you are in; keep in it. God will be worshipped in spirit and truth, in body and in soul. He will have both inward love and fear, and outward reverence of body and gesture.'

CHAPTER THREE

Darvell Bruderhof

WE HAD only been a short while at the Darvell Bruderhof, but already it felt as though we had been there some days or even weeks. The frenetic, crowded coming and going of London's Waterloo Station that we had left behind only a few hours before seemed far away indeed. Here at the Bruderhof we might have been in a different world; as indeed we were.

As we swung in through the gates and up the drive, I was surprised to find the place so large. Later, as we strolled round the grounds of what had once been a sanatorium and now is home to this Christian community of 250 adults and children, it was as though we were in some small, secluded village, miles from anywhere. Actually it had only been a short four-minute drive from Robertsbridge railway station; Robertsbridge, in the south of England, a Sussex village, itself small in size.

Here on the 70 acres of land the Bruderhof own at Darvell there are no shops, but a school, a small farm, office buildings, workshops and houses of many different sizes and types. A man passed us carrying a large tray of sticky buns, baked in the community's own kitchens. It had been a warm summer's day and now in the late afternoon small groups had gathered on the lawns outside the family dwellings – women and children mostly, the women sitting chatting, some telling stories or reading to the younger children. Older children played together, some pushing each other to and fro on swings dotted here and there. All, we noticed, ran around barefoot, a few we came across were racing downhill on home-made go-carts, laughing, shouting to each other. There was lots of laughter.

On our walkabout that first afternoon, there were many greetings, too. 'Hallo, I'm Barbara.' 'This is Claudia, my daughter-in-law, mother of ten.' 'Hallo, I'm Jeremy, my mother's son.' Our hosts that first afternoon and throughout our stay were Marjorie and Amy Hindley. Marjorie, a widow, celebrating that year fifty-one years in the Bruderhof; Amy, her daughter, an adult member since 1973, after a period outside the community. That means that three of Marjorie's four children are now at Darvell. A third son lives in Australia with his family.

Marjorie and Amy took us to meet Annie, Jeremy's wife, and then on to the third Hindley household where we met Tim and Claudia.

Tim and Claudia have a large family, ten in all. As we climbed the
stairs to their apartment, there was the sound of a violin being
played, one of their children practising; in the sitting-room, four
others were sitting, intent on drawing, reading or writing. Claudia
was helping a fifth get ready for bed, and Tim welcomed us with a
cup of tea.

Hanna, their teenage daughter, sitting next to me on the sofa,
wondered whether there would be waffles and maple syrup for
supper that evening. This sparked off a conversation about the
difficulty of obtaining real maple syrup here in England. The
community's supply comes from a Bruderhof community in the
States. For a while though, Tim told us, they made their own maple
syrup at Darvell, tapping sycamore trees in their own grounds. 'We
had quite a small industry going. There was a lot of interest locally,
even an article in the local newspaper.'

By the time we left Tim and Claudia and their family it was just
about suppertime. Nearly all the meals are eaten communally in
a large dining-hall. Hanna must have been disappointed for we
did not have waffles and maple syrup that evening. Instead there
was fried chicken and beetroot, followed by those large home-baked
sticky buns.

It was halfway through the meal that I almost dropped my fork
in alarm. Up to that point there had been a quiet hum of subdued
chatter. This was suddenly broken by a loud male voice that came
from I didn't know where. Marjorie laughingly indicated that the

voice came from two tables away and from a young man who was addressing us through a microphone, discreetly placed on the table in front of him. The chatter had stopped now and all listened as he said he had been on the telephone that afternoon to Woodcrest Bruderhof in America's New York State and brought greetings from the community there. Later in the meal the mike, a roving one, was passed to a couple who had just returned from visiting that same community. They shared news of their visit. All this was 'family news', and there were nods and smiles, and now and then a burst of laughter. I noticed the three large clocks that hung over the doors leading to the kitchen. Each clock showed a different time, one the time at Darvell, the other the time at Woodcrest, a third the time in Manitoba. There are four Bruderhofs in America, one in England and one just starting up again in Germany, where the first Bruderhof was formed in 1920. These six communities make up one family and as far as practicable each community arranges its life to make this a daily reality. They are all members of the Hutterian Church named after Jacob Hutter, a Moravian, who was part of the wider Anabaptist movement, the radical 'left-wing' of the Reformation.

Prayer and Potatoes

THROUGHOUT the meal we had been served by a number of young men in their late teens, and at the end of the meal Chris, noticing that it was the men who were doing the washing up in the kitchen, went to help. As I left the dining-hall one of the older men joked, 'Women's lib would approve, I think.' We chatted for a while about the way the community is perceived by those outside. Its members know that some view the community as clinging to practices that are outdated, even archaic. Even their dress dates back partly to the student movement of Germany in the 1920s and partly, much further back, to an old Tyrolean peasant costume of the sixteenth century. The men and boys wear black trousers and braces and check shirts. It is the braces that makes the way they dress so distinctive. For formal wear they have black suits – suits with no buttons only hooks. The women wear white blouses with puffed sleeves underneath a bodice made of the same material as their midi-length gathered skirts. It is a peasant-like dress enhanced as such by the beards of the men, and by the polka-dotted kerchiefs that the women and teenage girls wear on their heads. Younger girls wear bonnets.

'You see that's how we got these braces . . .' Jeremy playfully pinged his as he made this remark. It came at the end of our first evening. We had just heard a number of personal histories – of how this and that person had become a member – and little by little, the history of the Bruderhof communities was told.

Kathleen, now in her eighties, told of how she first heard of the Bruderhof from her sister. 'They live on prayer and potatoes . . .' her sister told her. That was in 1934 and the first Bruderhof community was young then, only fourteen years old. That first Bruderhof's home was in Germany's Rhön mountains, and its founders were Eberhard and Emmy Arnold. Eberhard Arnold was a theological teacher, in touch with the student movement that arose in Germany following World War I – disillusioned young people, scarred by the war years, seeking an alternative life style to that of their parents' generation. The alternative that the Arnolds embraced and offered was different enough. It was to find a way of living together that made following the example and teachings of Jesus a practicable daily reality . . . not to worry about food or clothes or possessions, not to take up arms, to learn instead how to love one's enemy, and how to live in peace and harmony with sister, brother, neighbour and with all God's creation. To many Christian men and women of that period in Germany it was a compelling challenge.

At first those who responded lived with the Arnolds in a large house in the village of Sannerz in the Rhön district. Later a large farm was purchased in the Rhön mountains. That was in 1927. When Kathleen's sister came into contact with the community in 1934, it was through meeting one of the Arnolds' sons, Hardi. To avoid enforced membership of the Nazi movement, he had come to study in England. It was through Hardi and his brother, Heini, and other young Bruderhöfers coming to England in this way that others we met at Darvell that evening had also become members of the community: Stanley and Marjorie as well as Kathleen.

Becoming a member of the Bruderhof is a serious matter at any time; serious indeed for those who joined in the 1930s. Stanley, whose first experiences were of conditions at the Rhoen Bruderhof, shuddered somewhat as he recalled those days. Their slim diet was of gruel, black bread and whatever vegetables were available. 'I didn't know it was possible to be so taken up with thoughts about food,' said Stanley. Yet hunger was not a new experience for him. Before joining the Bruderhof he had been a member of an itinerant preaching group in England, the Tramp Preachers, and by no means always certain of where his next meal would come from. But at the Rhön Bruderhof, conditions were to worsen.

The beliefs and life style of the Bruderhof were in no way compatible with the new Nazi government; the community was dissolved by the Gestapo and three of its members imprisoned for three months. The rest were allowed to leave the country. Some came to England. As the war progressed, however, the position of the German members became increasingly difficult. They were considered by some as enemy aliens, and to protect the community the government decided it would be necessary to intern the Germans

among them for the duration of the war. The brotherhood, however, did not want to be split up in this way. Permission was granted for the whole community to leave if they could find a neutral country willing to take them. The only country willing to do so was Paraguay, which necessitated a hazardous wartime sea journey. A few English members stayed behind, and in 1942 founded the Wheathill Bruderhof in Shropshire, a forerunner to the present community in Sussex.

Eberhard Arnold died during these happenings in 1935. His loss and the early chequered history of the young community took its toll. But before his death Eberhard Arnold had established an association with Hutterite communities in the United States and Canada, an association which was to be of great significance in the years to come. Part of the Arnolds' spiritual formation had come from what they had read of earlier religious socialists, including the sixteenth-century Hutterites. In 1927 Eberhard Arnold discovered that the Hutterite communities had not died out as he had thought, but still existed in parts of the United States and Canada. Excitedly he set out to visit them. So close in spirit did he find himself to these Hutterite communities, that he began to consider the possibility of his community becoming a part of this older tradition. It avoided the danger of establishing a new sect. In 1930 Eberhard Arnold became an elder in the Hutterite Church and the Bruderhof in Germany a part of the Hutterian brethren.

A guest asked: Do you mean to say that the Bruderhof is God's will? *Eberhard Arnold*: Not the Bruderhof, but total community. What we have recognized as being important is the life Jesus lived with his disciples and the life of the first Church in Jerusalem. We see the prophetic Old Testament likewise as a Word from God that we should live together in Church community (Psalm 133), in peace and justice and joy, as the Apostle Paul puts it (Rom. 14:17). Our whole life is meant only humbly to suggest the way. (Meeting with guests, Rhoen Bruderhof, August 22nd 1935)

During the years that the Bruderhof were in Paraguay links with their Hutterian brethren in the United States and Canada became tenuous, not only because of distance, but because differences arose concerning life style. Membership of the Hutterite Church was formally dissolved, but was restored in 1974 through the efforts of Eberhard Arnold's son, Heini. By then the Bruderhof had discovered once again that there was much wisdom in the ways of their older brethren, who were more experienced at living in community. The Bruderhof asked the forgiveness of the Hutterite brethren, and as a sign of repentance for the hurt they had caused, once again adopted the dress of the Hutterites. Jeremy's braces had told their story. His wife, Annie, had filled in parts of the story for us. As a child she had grown up in one of the Hutterite communities in South Dakota.

In the room that evening the gathering spanned four generations of Bruderhofers; the newest member, Hans Peter, a young man from Germany. Then there were visitors, including Chris and myself. There are nearly always visitors at a Bruderhof. You are welcome if you are genuinely interested in their life. While you are there you will be drawn into the community's life and that, incidentally, will include daily work. As they see it, it is not possible to have a shared life without shared work.

Daily Work and Play

DURING the week the community's day begins at 7.15 a.m. with breakfast. This is one of the meals that is eaten in families. I ate with Jeremy and Annie and their young daughter. Jeremy fried eggs for us all, and I continued to ask interminable questions.

Work begins at 8 a.m., and there is plenty to do. The community supports itself financially, and its main source of income comes from the manufacture and sale of children's toys and playthings, and of equipment for the handicapped. The workshop, built by the community with some outside help, is an extension of an old boiler house. We came here first on our tour of the community's buildings. Forty or more of the men work an eight-hour day, and if business is brisk, work may extend into the evening and others in the community, sisters as well as brothers, will come to help.

In the first section of the workshop, several older brothers were working, sewing foam blocks by machine. There is no redundancy at a Bruderhof. The older men – some in their late sixties, others in their seventies or eighties – work as many hours as they wish each day. There is no requirement for them to do so, but they like to do it.

Brightly-coloured foam blocks, hollow play blocks in weather-resistant non-toxic wood, slides, ladders, playmats, seesaws, carts, wagons, wheelbarrows, all are made here. Slightly more expensive we learnt than some children's playthings, but so hard-wearing that satisfied customers continually bring in more customers. Their equipment for the physically handicapped is for adults as well as children.

> Anything that is to have value must have a massive foundation. Unless we have community in the body, in things material, we will never have it in spiritual matters. We are not spirits; we are men of flesh and blood. Every day we need to eat; we need clothing for every season. We must share our tools, we must work together, we must work communally and not each for himself; otherwise we can never become one in the love of Christ. (C.F. Blumhardt, *Joy in the Lord*, p.61)

While the men are making playthings, some of the women work in the archives. Most of their work has to do with recording and preserving the community's history, also translating the writings of Eberhard Arnold and some of the early Hutterites into various languages. Here, too, the older women work as many hours as they wish, some in their seventies learning for the first time to use a word processor. 'How have you found it?' I asked one great-grandmother, admiring her skill. 'At first a little difficult,' she admitted, 'but fine now that I'm used to it.'

We next went to the schoolrooms. The Bruderhof run their own schools, educating their children to the age of fourteen; at Darvell, sixty-five children in eight grades. They have their own curriculum, the same in all five communities. Their aim is to draw out the natural creativity of each child, and to encourage disciplined learning habits. At fourteen the children go to state schools, and usually after that to college or university. Bruderhofers have learnt from experience that it is important that the choice to become an adult member of the community is a real choice, made only after there has been adequate time to experience life outside a Bruderhof. Their experience is also that their children gain from these years in a Bruderhof school; nearly all do well in state school examinations and at university. Even those who transfer from a Bruderhof school in America to the state system in England, have no difficulty fitting in

with educational standards, Amy told us. She is one of the teachers at Darvell. To teach in a Bruderhof school does not necessarily mean that you are a professionally qualified teacher. What is considered essential is the rapport you have with the children. It is the teacher–pupil relationship that is all important, as well as adequate knowledge of the subject you are teaching.

The school building at Darvell is bright, airy and colourful; its equipment up to date. Academic subjects are covered in the mornings, afternoons given more to arts and crafts. It was holiday time when we visited, so the buildings were mostly empty. Hanna, however, was there, teaching some of her younger sisters how to bake cookies. In one classroom we oohed and aahed over stick insects in a tank, and I noticed on the wall posters describing the steps set out in Betty Edward's *Drawing on the Right Side of the Brain*, a way of learning to draw that utilises the creative right side of the brain. For the uninitiated that is a technique I have used myself, fairly successfully! There is nothing old hat or boring about a Bruderhof education I decided.

After the school house, the baby house. That was not empty, but as it was sleep time our visit was brief. In order to allow the married women with children to take a full part in the shared work of the community, others care for the babies during work periods. For the majority of the women their daily work is in the kitchens or laundry or in the sewing room. There are also more women teachers than men. This is a rather sharp division of labour. There are no women elders. One or two of the women have started to work alongside

the men in their workshop, and there is usually one man working in the kitchen to hump the heavier pots and pans about. The one place where work is equally shared between women and men is in the administrative offices.

Our tour ended at the Brotherhood Room near to the dining-hall. Here the community gathers for its members' meetings and on Sundays for worship. Here, too, if the weather is wet, adult baptisms are conducted; if fine, these are conducted outside. Adult baptism marks full adult membership of the community. But first a member undertakes a period as a novice. This is of indeterminate length. 'It could be any length of time. It depends on the person. When they know they are ready to take the step, they ask for baptism.' His or her request is then considered by the whole brotherhood. Five young men were being prepared for baptism during the time that we visited.

The Wonder of Life

THE tour had taken the whole morning. Now it was time for lunch. The men break for two hours; the women for three. This long lunch-break enables families to spend time together, mothers to be with their children for an extended time. Family units though do not only consist of parents and children. Single people are always included. A number of the retired brothers, some widowed, live near to each other in a single-storey block, each with a separate room, but forming a family unit. One or more of the young men in the community also live as part of this unit, to be on hand for those who may need special assistance. The newest member, Hans Peter, whom we had met the night before, had done this for a while, and spoke of the wonder to him of forming deep relationships with those so much older.

Our tour ended, I had more questions than when we started. That afternoon Chris and I went to visit Ron and Emily. My first question was, 'What about marriage? Isn't choice a bit limited for a Bruderhofer? Presumably to stay a member, you need to marry a member.' As it happened it was an appropriate question to ask Ron and Emily. An older couple, they had only been married a few months. Ron, a widower for the last twelve years, Emily, up to that point single. Choice may be limited, but there are many marriages that do take place. Nevertheless, seeking it is not to be considered a priority; doing the will of God is. Ron said:

> You know, there are only two promises we make on our entry into adult membership. One is to seek to be a true disciple of Jesus Christ. The other is that our lives will be at the service of each other, as brothers and sisters. All other things are secondary to that. Marriage is important, but it is not all important.

It was the same kind of answer I had been given by Amy when I

asked her about career limitation. There are only certain jobs to be done at a Bruderhof, and members do not work outside, unless from economic necessity. '. . . but you see my concern is how can I best serve my brothers and sisters here. That's my motivation for work,' was her reply.

'It's not that important you know . . .' was a phrase that was repeated several times. Members do not have any money of their own, nor do they choose their own clothes. 'It's not that important . . .' There is a steward in charge of the community's purse; if you go out to buy food or household items or are away travelling on the community's business, you ask for what you need and then give an account when you return. Clothes are made in the community's sewing rooms, or purchased for you. 'If I need a pair of shoes, I tell the sister who buys them,' Ron told us. 'She knows my size.'

Perhaps I looked doubtful at the thought of someone else buying shoes for me, because Emily added, smiling, 'We really do care for one another. When I got married the sisters came and went through my wardrobe. They wanted to make sure I had clothes I would like. We know each other so well, they didn't need to ask me what I'd like.' And Ron added, laughing, 'Everyone knows I love ice-cream, and if I'm on a business trip, there's money for that, too.' Ron and Emily have been on several business trips together since their marriage.

This was the community's way of making sure they had some time away together, being newly-weds; another sign of caring.

'It's not that we are killjoys,' Stanley was to tell us later. 'Art, literature, all these things are valued by us. They are just not the centre of our life.' The community finds many ways to celebrate together. Just a week before our visit there had been a big celebration – a kind of funfair with side-shows, music and games. From what we heard adults had enjoyed it as much as the children.

The children learn in school how to handle money and there are opportunities as they grow older to spend it. In this way they prepare for life outside. Having a small sum of money to go and spend at a local market is an occasion. Life for a child growing up in a Bruderhof is very different from that of most children, but the impression made on a near-by neighbour is telling enough. One of the Darvell Bruderhof's neighbours was the writer and broadcaster, Malcolm Muggeridge. 'The children . . . give special delight; their eyes express the wonder of life rather than the fantasies of a TV screen; and their voices, when they sing, harmonise with the birds,' he has written.

What is Important

'IT'S NOT that important . . .' This oft-repeated phrase was never said heavily; more usually it was accompanied by an amused chuckle. The members of this community are not an over-serious people. They don't use a lot of overtly religious language; indeed this strictly 'religious' side of their life is a bit hidden. They say or more often sing grace at meals – often breaking out into incredible four-part harmonies; meals are also accompanied by reading aloud letters from other communities or from members away on mission journeys, or reports of world news or articles of interest from magazines. On Sundays there are prayers, songs and readings from the gospels or from the writings of Eberhard Arnold or the early Hutterites at the end of their family meeting. Prayer is a part of their life, but it seems less time is spent praying together than in some Christian communities.

> Our life will become not narrower, but broader; not more limited, but more boundless; not more regulated, but more abundant; not more pedantic, but more bounteous; not more sober, but more enthusiastic; not more faint-hearted, but more daring; not worse and more human, but filled with God and ever better . . . All this is Jesus and his Spirit of free-dom! He is coming to us. (Eberhard Arnold, from a letter, July 1922)

What is emphasised is *how* they live together. They know from experience that what kills community is gossiping, grumbling, complaining and backbiting. Their answer to this is to encourage a robust forthrightness with one another as part of caring. If there is a complaint, it is voiced. But only once. There is no going over the same ground time and again. They expect and receive frankness, but not the harbouring of resentment or of some petty irritation. If there is a serious disagreement between two or more members, others will help them sort it out. That they have and maintain unity as a community is at the heart of their lives. It is here that members talk of some of the inner, personal struggles; the struggle to be open, to be honest. In corporate decision-making, too, they seek the same kind of unity. Major decisions are taken only with the agreement of all the members. This kind of consensus can only be reached, we were told, by all being willing to listen to any dissenting voice and by anyone in disagreement with the others being brave enough to say so, perhaps to be the only one to do so. 'And more often than not, it's that person who's right,' Emily told us.

Some people find this life too hard, and leave. If they do, the community will do what it can to help them make a start elsewhere, but it is not obliged to return any money or possessions that were given to the community on that person's entering. There are also occasions when a member is given leave of absence from the community to work through some personal struggle – to come to grips with whatever in his or her life is making it too hard to live with others in community. Stanley had such a period outside the community, and returned. Now he says, 'Our understanding is that Jesus's call is to a life that is shared. If you come into community with any other understanding, you are going to come unstuck. If that is your understanding, then you can work through the hard times.'

Many of those we spoke to had joined the community because they had been seeking just such a communitarian Christian life-style and had not found it in their own churches, and sometimes not in other Christian groups or communities. Some had sought such an experience through membership of organisations for peace or social justice and likewise not found what they wanted. This was particularly the case with a number of the older members, now in their sixties and beyond. It was the case for Kathleen, Marjorie and Stanley. A more recent member, a young woman I worked beside folding clothes in the laundry, told me she and her husband had joined within the last few years. They had belonged to a charismatic prayer group and had tried living as an extended family with another couple from the same group, but the arrangement had not lasted. Many, therefore, of those who join already know how demanding such a community life can be, and are drawn to a community that has had years of experience working it out in practice. A struggle it may be to live this way, but many of the children growing to adulthood in a Bruderhof choose as adults to return. ('How do you do it?' a Jewish kibbutz member wants to know. Their experience has not been so positive, and they have invited some Bruderhofers to come and share their experience.) 'Well, sometimes it hasn't been that way,' Amy told us. There have been times in the history of the Bruderhof when life has become fractured and relationships fraught. 'That's when people begin to leave, and few return.' She is one, however, who has returned. 'Where else would I find a place where I can give myself so completely to my sisters and brothers, and where change is possible?'

To prove that such a life is possible is how the Bruderhofs see their calling. 'It's for the world that we exist, not for any other reason,' is the way Stanley put it. 'We want to show that it is possible to live a life that is based on serving others, not yourself. That's the way life is meant to work, and that's something the world needs to discover.'

CHAPTER FOUR

Franciscan Friary

I FOUND myself sitting with a plateful of pizza and baked potato balanced somewhat precariously on my knees, talking to a young woman who told me she worked for the BBC as a programme researcher for Radio 4 documentaries. She told me she had recently been to India, had hoped to meet the Dalai Lama, the spiritual leader of Tibet, but had just missed him. We talked about the Dalai Lama's recent appearance on British television, and she told me what an impression he had made on all the BBC staff who had met him. We were chatting together in the small sitting-room of the Franciscan Friary in London's East End. It did not, however, seem out of place to be talking about a Buddhist monk, the spiritual leader of Tibet. Certainly not in this evening's gathering.

Turning from my conversation with the programme researcher to talk with the young woman on my other side, I discovered she was a concert pianist, and freelancing most of the time like myself. We talked about the difficulties of freelance work. Looking around the room at the fifteen or so of us squashed together, some still standing, most squatting on cushions on the floor, I decided that the three of us sitting together were probably fairly typical of the group gathered – a writer, a researcher and a concert pianist. Most seemed to have come some distance across London to be here in London's East End. I met only two who lived nearby, one a woman who told me she worked for a shipping company several blocks away. We women outnumbered the men present.

This meal in the small Franciscan Friary in Stepney followed the regular Wednesday evening celebration of Holy Communion, a weekly event open to friends. Some were there because they felt at home here in this Friary, but were somewhat at odds with the Church otherwise. Here they had found a place where they could talk freely about their difficulties with the institutional Church, and their struggles to find a way to follow Jesus that was authentic for them. That evening there was no formal discussion, but conversation continued in small groups for an hour or so. Gradually the 'congregation' drifted away, and only Chris and I were left as the two guests staying at the Friary.

In contrast to other larger communities we were visiting, we had decided to come this time to one of the smaller Anglican Franciscan houses, in this case their first joint house of brothers and sisters together. At the time of our visit the four making up this small community were (brothers) Victor and Terry, (sister) Elizabeth, and Gillie, a novice sister. That first evening, the other guests gone, the six of us sat together and over large mugs of tea, talked about the following day. Terry was going to visit his mother in Kent; Victor had a work colleague coming to see him after Morning Prayer and then would be off to his part-time job as development officer for the Bishop of Stepney's lay training scheme; Gillie, a doctor, told us she was working half the day at the medical clinic; and Elizabeth said she had work to do preparing for the coming general chapter at Hilfield Friary in Dorset, an event at which all the brothers and sisters from the different houses in Britain gather annually. In between, the four said that they would find time to spend with Chris and myself, and as usual the day would be interspersed with times of prayer (offices) common to all the Franciscan houses. We said Compline together before going to bed earlyish, for the next day would begin with Morning Prayer at 7.15 a.m.

'Very Franciscan'

'**F**OR A few days we tried doing some physical exercises together after our half-hour of silent prayer, but only one or two of us really got into that, so we dropped it.'

It was the next morning, and the office of Morning Prayer had been followed by thirty minutes of silent prayer, and then Holy Communion. There were a few chairs in the room set aside as a chapel, but we knelt throughout on the thin cushions provided. All of us needed to move around and stretch arms and legs half-way through.

A local priest had come in to celebrate Communion, there being no priest within this small community. I noticed the changes that had been made to some of the wording within the daily office book we used – changes made lightly in pencil. '. . . *sons* of God' had been changed to 'children of God'; '. . . *he* who loves God is born of God and knows God' to '. . . those who love are born of God and know God'. Had these changes been agreed by the Chapters of the Society of St Francis, I asked? Yes, after much discussion, I was told. 'We haven't yet got round to tampering with God *himself* though,' Victor added, smiling.

Throughout the very informal breakfast ('Help yourself to cereal or toast or whatever you'd like . . .'), we continued to talk about the growing awareness within at least parts of the Church to the need to change its sexist language, and to find ways to affirm the fact

that God cannot be confined to either male or female descriptions. Breakfast over, everyone departed. The only matter of daily business to discuss was which room would be best for the visiting priest to use to sit and read in until lunchtime. For many of the local clergy the Friary provides such a place of quiet, away from their own telephones and doorbells.

The doorbell at 10 Halcrow Street, however, rings often; the telephone even more frequently. For its regular occupants life is very different from the more ordered life of a larger friary. The kind of order and regularity to be found at Hilfield Friary or at Compton Durville, the sisters' house in Somerset, is impossible here. There are no bells to remind whoever is at home that it is time for one of the four daily offices. Instead Elizabeth runs upstairs to ask Gillie, who is cooking the supper, whether she is ready to say Evening Prayer. On more than one occasion while we were there, only one of the sisters or brothers was at home to say the office. Chris and I joined in as best we could, not familiar with the way things were done. Saturday is a relaxed day and usually none of the offices is said corporately then.

At No. 10, there are also only four pairs of hands to do many tasks. On the Wednesday evening, Chris and I arrived rather inconveniently only fifteen minutes before the service was due to start. Elizabeth opened the door to us, greeted us warmly enough, but explained she was in the middle of a telephone conversation and rushed back to the phone. Left to our own devices, we brought our luggage in and then wandered upstairs. Up one flight and we were met by Victor, hurrying between the kitchen and sitting-room, pizzas in hand. Would we like a cup of tea? In the circumstances, we declined. Victor shouted for Terry to show us to our rooms. Chris had to struggle up to the 'top-top' with all his photographic equipment; the house a typical Victorian terraced house four storeys up with

only one or two rooms on each floor. By now the doorbell was ringing constantly.

In the midst of all this busyness, the chapel is a quiet place. An ordinary living-room, the walls painted a pale magnolia; in the fireplace two large pieces of roughly-cut grey stone, an icon, some candles; in front a table, more candles, and beneath the table, a green fern. Above over the fireplace, a crucifix, the figure of a black Christ, its cool, simple but striking lines compelling one to look and reflect. In the corner to one side, another table with a candle placed on it and the traditional figure of Francis, cross in hand. At the foot of the table, a geranium, a bright splash of red. Looked at more closely this table was in fact only three pieces of wood balancing rather precariously on one another. 'Very Franciscan' was Elizabeth's laughing comment as she pointed this out to us. The 'top-top' attic room with its large picture windows is another quiet place. This is usually where guests stay who come for a time of retreat.

'Very Franciscan', too, are the names that have stuck in this friary for who does what and for their regular house meetings. There is no named person in charge, but one of the four is IT for the week, chairing the weekly diary meeting and keeping a kind of an eye on tasks being done and offices said. Terry was IT for the week Chris and I were at the friary. IT is shared in alphabetical order or almost alphabetical. Elizabeth is away a lot, and that makes a bit of a hiccup in the system. House meetings are given high priority, 'more important than anything else', and are marked in red in their diaries. They are seen as essential to 'making community'. As well as the weekly diary meeting, there is a monthly meeting to deal with 'nuts and bolts', and then US, a time to get together 'to talk about ourselves, what's going on inside or between us', and DIVINITY . . . 'well, that's about us and God'.

This friary is not the only one to have no named person in charge, but all the larger friaries have guardians. Guardians are elected by chapter. The chapters are elected from the fully pro-fessed brothers or sisters, and meet to make decisions that affect the whole family. Each province has one for sisters and one for brothers.

A Bit Like Topsy

TO VISIT this friary amid the urban poverty of London's East End is to return to where the community of St Francis began in the early 1900s. Its earlier roots go back of course to Assisi in the twelfth century, and to Francis himself. It was a special devotion to Francis – the rich man, voluntarily turned poor – that led Sister

Rosina, fifteen years a member of the Anglican community of the
Sisters of Bethany, to change direction in her forties and to gather
a few women around her to seek to follow more exactly the example
of Francis, in particular that of voluntary poverty and service of the
poor. Sister Rosina was at the time, 1905, working in the parish
of Holy Redeemer, Clerkenwell, in the East End. Her community
released her to follow her inclination, and she and the few women
with her began to seek a place to put into practice her ideas. 'Our
community has always been like this,' said Elizabeth. 'People have
an idea and it's perhaps taken up and tried. A bit like Topsy in the
way it has grown.'

At that period the Church of England was still uncertain whether
it approved of religious houses. A good number of Anglican communities had begun to spring up from the mid-nineteenth century; and
though finding some difficulty in gaining recognition, they had often
proved themselves in their works of caring. A priest in Hull invited
Sister Rosina and her group of women to come and work among the
poor in his docklands parish. This they did for three years, taking
in washing as a way of earning their living, and spending their time
visiting the poor around them. In 1908 the Bishop of London invited
the group back to London to work in Dalston, where they opened a
home for the elderly sick.

Elizabeth herself joined the community in 1955 when it was still
in Dalston. In 1962 it moved out of London to Compton Durville in
Somerset about 20 miles from the brothers' first English house. Well
before then the brothers had started their community, or rather an
amalgamation of several. As with the sisters, the brothers' growth
was ragged and unpredictable. Perhaps more so, as during this
period a number of small Franciscan-type groups had started in
different parts of the country. Eventually it was an Anglican priest,
Father Algy Robertson, who drew these groups together to form
the Society of St Francis. That was in 1937. From the start the
brothers were more in number than the women, and the founding
of the Society helped the women's community in its growth. In
1964 it adopted the same constitution as the brothers. From this
uncertain early growth, the Society of St Francis has grown to
include now fourteen houses in Britain alone, and three autonomous
overseas provinces in Australia, New Zealand, the Pacific Islands
and America.

There have been many changes over the years. Things were
beginning to change, Victor said, when he joined the Society
seventeen years ago. But he has memories prior to this of being a
guest in a friary, and of '. . . all the brothers putting their hoods up
as they left the chapel after Compline, and of their disappearing then
for the night.' All this has changed. While we were at the Friary,
the sisters and brothers dressed in ordinary, everyday clothes, and
only appeared once or twice in their brown Franciscan habits, and

sat around chatting informally late into the evening. The biggest change, however, Victor said, has been in the changed relationship between the women's and men's communities.

Until comparatively recently the women's community had to be under the protection of the men's, or before that of a male visitor. Now it has its own independent existence within the Society. Elizabeth is the minister provincial for the European Province. The idea of a joint house came when the Society held a 'Gospel Now' conference to reflect together as a worldwide Society how the good news that Jesus brought could work today for them and others. Discovering a new way of women and men relating and working together was one thing which came out of the conference. The Society already had 'mixed houses' – sisters working and living alongside the brothers in one of their houses, a brother part of the women's community at Newcastle-under-Lyme. A joint house, however, was something different. It has been in existence now for six years.

Did such a closer relationship between religious women and men make it more difficult to live the celibate life, I asked Victor. He thought for a moment and then recalled a conversation he had had with an old nun some years back. She, he said, had just moved from

a large convent where she had been enclosed behind high walls, to a smaller house where there were no walls, and she had said to him, 'The vow of celibacy is pretty meaningless when you are so well protected, but it begins to take on meaning when you are not.' His experience, he said, was similar to hers. Living in a less protected environment meant you really had to *choose* to live the vow of celibacy daily, and 'it is only in choosing it that it is yours'. Living in any small house, he said, had this effect, whether mixed, joint or otherwise. 'It's because you have to share your life on a much closer, everyday level.'

'But it does take a certain kind of maturity,' said Elizabeth.

Taking Vows

WHILE showing us round the neighbourhood, Gillie also talked to us about her time as a novice sister. It usually takes three years before a novice can consider taking the next step to becoming a fully-blown 'religious'. The next step is to take 'first vows'. Final vows may then be taken between three and seven years. Gillie, having been a novice for three years, was needing to make her decision to stay or leave the Society. 'A lot of people do leave having completed their time as a novice. But first vows, that's a more serious commitment . . .'

What had drawn her to the Franciscans in the first place, I asked? Gillie explained that in her teens she had been interested for a while in the Buddhist religion, then at university had become a member of an evangelical Christian group. This had been too extrovert and 'upfront' for her. So for one of her long vacations she decided to try something different, and woke up one morning with the thought that she would like to go and stay for a while in a convent. This she did; not a Franciscan convent at that point, but the visit awakened an interest in the religious life. It led her to seeking out and developing friendships with a number of Franciscan brothers, first in Cambridge, then later in London's East End. By that time she was a qualified doctor, but also seriously considering becoming a Franciscan sister. 'It bugged me enough, I guess, for me *to have* to look at this possibility seriously.' She was uncertain as to whether she should go on to take first vows, but she rather thought she might. On the other hand, she loved her work as a GP, and to continue to combine the two . . .?

Taking final vows for the brothers and sisters means affirming a call to a life of poverty, chastity and obedience. These are what they call their three conditions of life. There are also three ways by which they serve God: prayer, sacred study (by which is meant primarily study of the Scriptures and of the lives of the saints), and practical works. The practical works start first of all at home with the ordinary menial tasks of cleaning, dusting, cooking and washing up, and of weeding and planting out in the garden (only at No. 10 there is no garden to tend), and extends outside in ministry, particularly to the uncared-for, the sick, the suffering and the needy. All this is to be done in a spirit of humility, love and joy; if these are lacking then the point of living as religious together is lost and becomes in their words, 'unprofitable and barren'. 'What do I need to bring with me?' a young woman, interested in joining the Society, asked one of the earlier mothers. 'Your common sense and your sense of humour,' she was told. It is still considered good advice.

Francis of Assisi insisted that those who joined him as friars first dispossessed themselves of whatever money or possessions they had by distributing these among the poor. Today's brothers and sisters also have to dispossess themselves – giving to their family or to charity as they see fit, but only at life profession. On entry they 'freeze their assets' in an account with bank or building society in case they later decide to leave the Society. Whatever clothes or material goods are acquired after that as necessary to their daily life and work are the common possession of the community, not of the individual. In this they are renouncing 'a self-reliant and independent existence in favour of mutual give and take', a sharing of common resources. It does not mean that a brother or sister cannot have the personal use of, say, a book or radio, but it is not their own possession – and someone else's need may be greater! Sitting lightly to material goods is also behind the Society's rule that it does not own property; and avoids acquiring large funds. In this way they are kept dependent on God, and more at his disposal.

The Prayer of St Francis

Lord, make us instruments of your peace
Where there is hatred, let us sow love;
Where there is injury, pardon;
Where there is doubt, faith;
Where there is despair, hope;
Where there is darkness, light;
Where there is sadness, joy.

O Divine Master, grant that we might not so much seek
 to be consoled as to console,
 to be understood as to understand,
 to be loved as to love.
For it is in giving that we receive, in pardoning that we are
  pardoned, and in dying that we are
 born to eternal life. Amen.

The vow of chastity is again not a negative choice, of forsaking marriage only, but a choice to seek and nurture deep and trusting friendships with many people, friendships that are not possessive or exclusive, and that help to bring about growth and maturity, your own and that of the other person. As Victor emphasised, to choose celibacy is not a choice you make just once, but one that you continue to choose as you are confronted with different circumstances. It is also necessarily a call from God – 'love for whom makes it possible'.

Obedience is not blind obedience. Francis taught that obedience was to God, to a continual conversion, to a way of life similar to that of Jesus himself, and that no friar was to obey an order that went against his own conscience or the teachings of Jesus. One's own conscience, however, can at times be an uncertain guide, and

to open oneself to others' opinions and judgement considered an essential part of the process of discerning what is best not just for oneself but also for the whole community. Getting the right balance is something that the Society has to work at continually. Such discernment includes decisions about where brothers or sisters will live and what work they will do, but they are freer now than they were in the past to state their preferences or to pursue concerns or interests of their own.

This interpretation of the vows is for those in what is called the First Order. The Society has a Second Order, the Order of St Clare, for sisters who are called to a more enclosed life of prayer. They have a house, St Mary's Convent, in a small village outside Oxford. Then there is the Third Order. This is for men and women in secular life, married and single, who want to live the Christian life under the same vows, adapted and annually renewed, and who are drawn to follow as closely as they can the example of Francis in this. Prayer, compassion for the poor and the marginalised, avoiding luxury and waste, living joyfully, all this is involved.

Francis, an Enigma

'THERE are so many facets to Francis's character,' Elizabeth said to us as we ate lunch with her and Gillie on our last day. 'People know of course about his work with lepers and his love of animals and birds, but perhaps not much beyond that. He was so human, so full of humour, had such an appreciation of life, such a respect for all whom he met.' It was this respect for all people and his appreciation of life that led Francis to be not only a friend of the poor, but also a peacemaker. He was perhaps the first multi-faith dialogist, entering into respectful dialogue with the head of that day's Muslim community and risking his own life to do so in an attempt to bring peace between Christian and Arab.

We were talking about living the Franciscan ideal today. Francis's example is relevant indeed to the friary in Stepney, situated as it is in a poor neighbourhood and where there are also many Muslim families. Recent development of this part of London's East End, its docklands, has done little to alleviate the poverty in which most of its inhabitants live, the majority of the more recent arrivals from Bangladesh. The close-knit East End community that once lived here has gone now, replacing it is a strange mix, not only of colour and race, but of the very rich and the very poor, or as one local put it to us, 'a mixture of Perrier water and brown ale'. Those who drink the Perrier water live in the newly developed penthouse flats along the river-bank, that sell for £500,000 or more. The growing gentrification of their neighbourhood daily threatens the security of the locals, as Gillie has discovered.

Lately I've noticed how many of the old people when they get sick, seem to die much quicker here than elsewhere. They don't have much will to live, with so little security. When I first came here it didn't seem as bad as I imagined it would be, but after a while I realised it was worse. That's when I began to understand the circumstances that most people live in and how little they can hope for, how few options they have.

Gillie was most in daily contact with neighbourhood people. Elizabeth's work does not leave her much time to do so. Victor's job is for East End folk, but a good deal of it is administrative. Terry is a member of the Labour Party, serves on the local Community Health Council and does some part-time evening work at the local postal sorting office, but felt embarrassed that his contact with local people was limited.

Yet service of the poor is what most Franciscans are thought to be about. Terry and I talked about this, and about the questions that serving the poor pose for many Christians today. How is this to be done when merely alleviating needs can be a way of perpetuating social inequality? To help himself and others consider this challenge Terry has started a justice and peace group for Franciscans. He believes also that there is a pressing need today for Christians to find a way of praying that helps them meet this challenge, the kind of praying that both brings about repentance for social sin and creates hope for a different future. Today's Franciscan brothers and sisters give a large amount of their time to helping other Christians develop and deepen just such a relevant spirituality; Elizabeth, Victor and Terry all do so. And today's intake of new novices also relates to this search for a new spirituality, Victor told me. 'At the time when I joined most of us were drawn by the social caring side of Franciscan life, but many of today's novices are on a more spiritual quest.' He saw this as paralleling needs in society itself, a search on the part of many for new meaning and fresh hope.

Service of the poor and the marginalised remains, however, a practical need to be met, and this happens albeit informally in a number of different ways at No. 10. Some of those who come may be local priests seeking a place of quiet, or middle-class professionals bringing along their questions about the Church and faith and daily life, but there are others, too, with more particular needs, burnt-out or not-so-burnt-out schizophrenics, out-patients from a nearby hospital. One 'regular' was settled comfortably in the sitting-room when Chris and I first arrived, and greeted us with a nod of his head, but was otherwise silent. He continued to sit there while the rest of us went downstairs for the service in the chapel, but roused himself to help wash up dishes after the meal. 'I expect he's already taken Communion elsewhere today,' Terry told us. 'He does the round of nearly all the local churches daily.'

For the Order

At the Chapter General of the Order at Whitsun 1220, Francis resigned further responsibility for ruling the Order: 'Henceforth I am dead to you. But here is Brother Peter Cattani whom we all, you and I, will obey.' Whereupon he bowed down before him and promised him obedience and reverence. The brothers then began to weep; great was their grief on seeing themselves as it were abandoned as orphans. Francis clasped his hands and raising his eyes to heaven said:

To you, Lord, I commend this family
which you committed to my care until today.
By reason of my infirmity, which you know,
my sweetest Lord,
I can no longer sustain the care of it.
I commend it also to the Provincial Ministers;
they will answer for it
at the day of judgement
if any brother, by their negligence
or by their bad example
or their too harsh correction,
should perish.

St Francis at Prayer

Struggles of living the Franciscan life today and coping with burnt-out schizophrenics, there were tales to tell and some funny anecdotes to relate. How is simplicity of life to be measured, for instance? The four occupants of No. 10 have had to struggle with this one, and with their different ideas about this. Should an old table bought at a junk-yard be replaced with a better one? They were offered a better one, and so took it. The drawers on a cupboard in the kitchen had no handles and had to be prised open with one's fingernails. Elizabeth particularly found this irksome, and there are handles now. There are also cushions to kneel or sit on in the chapel, and these were a comparatively new addition. We were glad of them.

Each friary aims to live at a level that supports work and good health, but which is as simple and as economical as possible. There is in fact little extravagance. Chris and I went to the local market with Elizabeth. Four pounds of mushrooms bought for £1 were quickly dealt with on our return, and were made up into little packets for the freezer. They would stretch for use in several stews. Houses are economically independent as far as possible, and share excess money with other more needy houses. Gifts and legacies along with earnings are the source of income for the Society. At No. 10 the allowance is put in an open kitty, and each person takes whatever he or she needs, filling in a chit to say the amount and purpose. They find they can keep their living expenses down to about £50 a week per person. Such economies make a celebration out of any unexpected luxuries. Chris and I bought some courgettes and strawberries at the market, and these added to a Spanish omelette and beans made a splash-up lunch, ice-cream being added as a special treat to eke out the strawberries. Victor had joined us by then, and he, Elizabeth and Gillie told us, amid chuckles, about the previous Christmas at the Friary. On Christmas Eve the nearby Sainsbury's had offloaded left-overs on to them, and there had been strawberries and cream for breakfast and orchids on the table. It was Elizabeth's first Christmas at the Friary, and Victor with a perfectly straight face had presented her with an orchid, telling her it was a household tradition that the sisters were each presented with an orchid on Christmas Day.

This not taking things too seriously, the ability to laugh together, to see the funny side, was perhaps what I most enjoyed and appreciated at No. 10. On our second evening Terry returned from his visit to his mother in Kent and solemnly unwrapped a gift she had sent ... several gingerbread men. 'Would you like an arm or rather have the head?' I was asked, as he dismembered the brown biscuits. There were only four, and seven of us. We crunched our way through the biscuits, recalling childhood memories of similar gingerbread men. A young woman had come to visit the Friary that evening. She was considering joining a religious order, and had come to talk to Elizabeth about what it would mean to become a Franciscan. 'I definitely like it here,' she said meaningfully to us all as she left. 'There's more to being a Franciscan than gingerbread men, though ...', said Gillie, restoring a sense of proportion.

Indeed, learning to live Francis's way is as demanding now as it has ever been.

Chapter Five

Iona

'HERE in Muirhouse life is very difficult for many people. One example is the single-parent families, many of whom live in bed and breakfast accommodation. Their hope of getting a council home is limited, and most of the single parents are unemployed. There is no work around here.'

We were driving through Muirhouse, a large housing estate on the outskirts of Edinburgh, a part of this festival city that is not shown in the tourist guides. It was here that we began our visit to the Iona Community, staying overnight in one of its Columba Houses before travelling on the next day to the island of Iona. This Columba House was not one house at all, but three small council flats on different levels in the same block – a 'stair community'.

We stayed with Margaret Wright on the middle level; below her are Helen and Alan, Emma, Kate and Christine, and above her Mary and Rhona and Alasdair. From 1976–81 Margaret was housekeeper at Iona Abbey, a job she found through an advertisement in *The Lady*. When she left, she returned to her previous home in Somerset, but missed the community so much, she moved to Muirhouse. 'I don't think it's a good idea to live alone,' she said.

Members of this 'stair community' eat supper together three evenings a week and lunch on Sundays, taking it in turn to provide the meal. We all ate together that evening in Margaret's flat; the children almost too excited to sit down and eat, as it was Hallowe'en and they were off to a party afterwards.

Nearby there is another Columba House. We did not visit that one, but later at Iona we met Diane Robertson, who was able to tell us about it. She is not a member of the Iona Community, but is of this Columba House; a mix of members and non-members is quite usual. 'At first I lived with one of the families, but now I've moved into my own flat in the same block,' she told us with evident glee. And with even more, '. . . but I'm back every evening knocking on the door asking them what they're having for supper, or what they're watching on television.'

'That's very true,' her friend nodded, laughing at her.

'Well I haven't lived on my own before,' said Diane, 'I'm having to learn.' She pressed me: 'You will put me in the book?'

'Probably I will,' I said.

A learner she might be at housekeeping, but twice a week she visits George MacLeod, the founder of Iona Community, and helps him with his housekeeping. He, too, lives in Edinburgh, a widower, and now in his nineties.

The Thin Place

IONA itself is a world away from Muirhouse. Margaret woke us at 6 a.m. in time to leave the flat by 7 a.m. To get to Iona that day we had to catch the 7.30 a.m. train from Edinburgh to Glasgow, and change at Glasgow on to the 8.35 a.m. bound for Oban. No fast inter-city train, but a stop-start, somewhat shabby, shunting and creaking its way north-east, then south again, Garelochhead, Tarbert, Ardlui, Crianlarich, Dalmally, Loch Awe, Falls of Cruachan – the station names alone are enough to draw one on.

There was no buffet on this train either ('not in the winter months', the ticket collector told us; we were travelling in late October). Luckily we had anticipated this possibility and bought coffee and doughnuts at Glasgow in the few minutes we had between trains. The slowness of the journey is more than bearable. To bury yourself in a book (my wont!) a shame, for soon you are cutting your way through heavily wooded slopes, magnificent even in late autumn, the trees fading ochre against a background of blue-green pines, and always in sight of water – a river, a loch or a mountain stream, white flecked. By the time we reach Oban, it is not only the train that is moving at a slower pace. I am glad we have come by train, rather than by car, and have begun to see that the journey itself is a preparation; to arrive at Iona too quickly would be to arrive too soon.

At Oban an hour's wait at the terminal before boarding the ferry that will take us across to the island of Mull. The crossing takes only forty minutes, and there is a dash to the cafeteria. A bowl of Scotch broth and a large plate of Scotch pie, chips and peas for under £2. 'I hope I won't regret it,' I say, as I sit down to my meal. I had been told the crossing could be rough midway. 'Oh no,' said a fellow traveller overhearing, 'with that pie inside you, you'll be fine. A good stabiliser.'

At Mull we disembark and there is a coach awaiting us, and a long 30-mile drive across the length of Mull to where another ferry will take us to Iona. The coach is spanking new and overwarm and I am lulled almost to sleep. Chris nudges me awake. 'There's Iona.' I can hardly make it out, a grey silhouette in the distance, and rather unpretentious. In contrast to Mull, Iona is only three miles long and a little over one mile in breadth. George MacLeod has called it 'a very thin place; only a bit of tissue paper between things material and things spiritual'.

Tantalisingly close now, but even so we do not know if we shall arrive there that day. Margaret Wright had warned us. 'It's unpredictable; it's weather permitting, and . . . well, other things.' Her departure from Iona had been delayed four times in one day, she told us. Each time the community had gathered at the quay to wave goodbye, and each time she had to return to the abbey. The weather was no problem this time, but the crew were occupied with what we hoped were minor repairs to the ferry, seemingly oblivious to those who had disembarked from the now departed coach. I could see Iona Abbey beckoning across the small slip of water, and it was with considerable relief that after a while we were allowed to board the ferry and cross.

Our visit took place at the end of the season, during a work week. A young woman who arrived at the same time, but was not expected, was delighted to be told she could stay at the Abbey without charge if she was willing to work and could stay the full time. Greeted and shown to our rooms, we pick our way over buckets and mops, and avoid the areas freshly painted. We are shown the library: a volunteer is dusting books. There are lots of winding steps and corridors leading in many directions. 'We are aware of the limitations for disabled people and families . . .' the information sheet for guests reads. A new centre has, however, just been built with additional facilities.

My room is small with a tiny window and two bunk beds. Outside volunteer workers chat their way through the afternoon's work. 'I never was good at cleaning windows.' 'I'd better stay and work a little longer, I haven't done much.' On the way to our rooms, Alison had pointed out the common room. 'There's a kettle there. You can make tea and coffee for yourselves at any time.' She also told us we should find our names on the list of daily chores. We are not part of the work week as such, but guests at all times help with chores. Chris finds he is on kitchen duty, and I am to help tidy the common room and serve lunch.

For the time that we are at Iona Abbey, we are a part of its community life, invited to make ourselves at home. In the Abbey itself, the accommodation is homely, simple, even a little shabby, but this makes it easier to sit around, talk, chat, play the piano, have a singsong. If you want to be alone and quiet, there is the library or the abbey church itself, a bit cold mid-autumn though.

Eating meals in the old abbey refectory, passing through the columned cloisters on the way in and out, attending the services morning and evening, all help to sustain the sense of this being a pilgrimage, which actually started back in Glasgow when one boarded the 8.35 a.m. train. And, indeed, as George MacLeod puts it, the Iona Community would not exist 'if there had not been a Govan'.

Columba

Columba's playmates called him Colum-cille (Column of the Church), which shows how as a boy he was fond of helping with the services and sharing in the work. To this day Gaelic-speaking people talk of him as Colum-cille. He loved the old poetic tales of his race, but he was also a very practical organiser, as may be guessed by the number of churches he founded; over three hundred in Ireland alone and many scores in Scotland. He always took his share in any work, and after months of strenuous labour he would retire to some quiet monastery and there recreate himself, reading the old tales, fasting and praying, and then off to action again.

But his favourite hobby was illumination, that is, copying and decorating the old manuscripts. One legend tells how he had made a beautiful copy of the Psalms from a manuscript belonging to his old master, Finnian. The old man claimed the copy as his, which roused the wolf-side of Columba, and the quarrel ended in a great battle with huge loss of life. Soon afterwards the dove-side of Columba showed him his mistake, and he decided to leave Ireland in remorse and win souls for Christ, instead of killing men in battle.

Another story explaining why Columba left Ireland tells us that some Irish settlers in Dalriada (which we know as Argyll) were defeated and crushed by King Brude of the Northern Picts and that one of Columba's relations was killed. This made Columba decide that the only way to unite these squabblers was the Christian way of Love and Friendship, so he came to Scotland to spread the story of Christ and unite the quarrelling tribes. (*The Story of Iona*)

Place of the Common Life

GOVAN is a part of Glasgow, at one time one of Britain's biggest shipbuilding centres. The depression of the 'thirties hit Govan particularly hard. George MacLeod was then a young Presbyterian minister, in charge of Govan old parish church. How to bring humanity back to a life that had gone 'sour and secular' was a question that perplexed him.

He began a mission of friendship, and with a team of volunteers visited homes and preached on street corners. This mission resulted in two hundred adults joining the church, and over two hundred children the Sunday school. That, he says, couldn't happen today, but even then the gap between the Church and ordinary people was beginning to widen.

'It was almost as though there was a wall around the church.' George MacLeod's answer to this was to move to the other side of the wall. He found an old ruined mill near Glasgow, and invited unemployed craftsmen to help repair it. Members of the Govan old congregation worked alongside them. 'What a brotherhood is born with unchurched workers when you talk with them instead of at them,' George MacLeod recalls.

How the church was to stay in touch with ordinary working people was of constant concern to George MacLeod. He began to envisage a 'brotherhood within the Church of Scotland, of no permanent vows, into which men of such a mind could come for the first two or three years of their ministry'. It was to be a new kind of training situation to prepare Church of Scotland ministers for urban ministry. After leaving theological college they would spend three months as part of a small resident community where they would live and work alongside skilled manual workers; at the end of that time they would move to parishes in urban areas, but still retain membership of the brotherhood. It was to be a more permanent Fingleton Mill situation, and the place that George MacLeod had in mind for this was Iona.

Iona has its own unique history as a launching-pad for mission. In the sixth century the monk Columba sailed from Ireland to Iona and established a monastic community there, and from this island he and his monks set forth on their many missionary journeys to parts of Scotland and Northern England. The community Columba founded existed until the ninth century when the monastery was ransacked by Viking invaders, and sixty-eight monks died. In the early thirteenth century Benedictines were invited to establish a new community on the site of the original Columban monastery. Parts of the present Abbey date back to this time, but the Benedictines were to depart after the Reformation. The memory of Iona as a holy place, however, remained; in the eighteenth century pilgrims began to visit the island. They and succeeding pilgrims clamoured for the Abbey to be rebuilt. The owner, the Duke of Argyll, gave the ruins to the Church of Scotland in 1899, under a deed of gift, and a board of trustees was set up. (The buildings are still owned by the Church of Scotland, and leased to the Iona Community.) In 1912 the sanctuary, the place of worship, was restored; the rest of the buildings still lay in ruins. 'Somebody ought to do something about that,' said George MacLeod on a visit to Iona. The 'somebody' was soon to become his new brotherhood.

Rebuilding the part of the Abbey that had been the monks' living quarters symbolised for George MacLeod the rebuilding of the common life. 'It's the place of the common life that's in ruins . . . the cities, the streets, the factories . . .' Learning how to live and share life together as part of a Christian community was what the Church needed to learn he felt, and what it had then to share with a world that knew even less about such a shared life.

In 1938 six ministers and six craftsmen began the job of rebuilding. Not a very large community at that point. When George MacLeod made a home movie of these early beginnings, members appeared and reappeared in different shots in order to make the community look larger. Gradually others came not only from Glasgow and other parts of Scotland, but eventually from all over the world. Many of them were labourers, skilled at their jobs, but uncertain about the church part. Nevertheless, George MacLeod insisted that all those who worked together also worshipped together, twice a day in the Abbey church.

Faith came alive in a new way for many, but that was not all that happened. The worship itself came alive in a new way. Old ways were challenged – saying 'thou' instead of 'you' – prayers became shorter and more to the point. A lively faith was needed. There were many setbacks and difficulties. On one occasion restoration work was threatened by a shortage of timber; it had all been requisitioned by the War Office. The problem was solved when a ship from Canada had to jettison her cargo of timber in a storm.

She was just opposite the mouth of the Clyde when this happened, and the timber floated eighty miles and landed on the coast of Mull, opposite Iona. Not only that, but it was all cut to the right lengths!

Such signs of God's grace are a part of the folklore of Iona. There are stories of miraculous healings and of a journey Columba made to Loch Ness and of his vanquishing with a word the Loch Ness monster who threatened him and his monks. 'Columba the Good' he was named. He apparently foresaw the day when his monks would depart and the buildings become ruins, but he also prophesied that 'before the world comes to an end, Iona will be as it was'.

By 1956 the work was almost complete. Queen Elizabeth II came to visit the Abbey, the first reigning monarch to do so since Margaret, Queen of Scots, in the eleventh century. Yet in its graveyard lie kings of Scotland, two kings of France and eight kings of Norway.

In 1959 the cloisters were opened and in 1966 the rebuilding was complete. The brotherhood was soon to be extended to include women as well as men, lay people as well as ordained. A new Iona Community had been born, a dispersed community, with its members living in many parts of Scotland and also in England and other parts of the world. Essentially, however, it is a community of Scots. The leader of community, at present John Harvey, does not live at Iona Abbey but in Glasgow and works from the community's mainland centre there. There is a community of residence on Iona, but it is small, only a dozen or so, who make up the island staff. Iona Abbey is the public face of the Iona Community; an important part of its work, but by no means all. 'It is a common misconception,' Alison Newall, the joint warden of the Islands, told us, 'that everything happens here.'

When the Lights Are On

Leader: When the lights are on
             And the house is full,
             And laughter is easy,
             And all is well . . .

Voice: Behold I stand at the door and knock.

Leader: When the lights are low
             And the house is still,
             And the talk is intense,
             And the air is full of wondering . . .

Voice: Behold I stand at the door and knock.

Leader: When the lights are off
And the house is sad,
And the voice is troubled,
And nothing seems right . . .

Voice: Behold I stand at the door and knock.

Leader: And tonight,
Always tonight,
As if there were no other people,
no other house,
no other door . . .

Voice: Behold I stand at the door and knock.

Leader: Come Lord Jesus, be our guest,
Stay with us for the day is ending.
Bring to our house your poverty

All: FOR THEN WE SHALL BE RICH.

Leader: Bring to our house your pain

All: THAT SHARING IT WE MAY ALSO SHARE YOUR JOY.

Leader: Bring to our house your understanding of us,

All: THAT WE MAY BE FREED TO LEARN MORE OF YOU.

Leader: Bring to our house all those
Who hurry or hirple behind you,

All: THAT WE MAY MEET YOU AS THE SAVIOUR OF ALL.

Leader: Bring to our house your Holy Spirit,

All: THAT THIS MAY BE A CRADLE OF LOVE.

Leader: With friend, with stranger,
With neighbour, with the well-known ones,
Be among us tonight,

All: FOR THE DOORS OF OUR HOUSE WE OPEN
AND THE DOORS OF OUR HEARTS WE LEAVE AJAR.

Leader: In our life and believing . . .

All: THE LOVE OF GOD.

Leader: At our end and new beginning . . .

All: THE ARMS OF GOD TO WELCOME US
AND BRING US HOME.   AMEN.
(The Iona Community Worship Book)

Hope Waits

IONA, however, is likely to be the place where most people first encounter the community. For the most part tourists have replaced pilgrims, and the community has a welcome for them, as well as for its own guests. Day visitors can join in a guided tour of the buildings, stop for a snack in the abbey coffee house or browse around the book and gift shop in the abbey cloister. On weekdays at 2 p.m. Monday to Saturday there is the opportunity to join in prayer in the abbey church. The prayers focus on the issues of justice and peace. To the community today's tourists are also pilgrims.

At the Abbey itself there are programmed weeks throughout most of the year; many of the weeks explore issues that are the corporate concern of the community: social justice, peace, community, celebration. Whatever the theme or topic of a particular week, the pattern of weekly services in the Abbey stays the same. On Mondays there is prayer for peace and justice, on

Tuesdays prayer for healing. The healing service on Tuesday
started as a result of the many requests that the community
received from members and visitors for prayer for the sick. The
emphasis is on prayer for wholeness of body, mind and spirit,
and of prayer for healing being the ministry of the whole Church.
The laying-on of hands that accompanies prayer for healing is
the action of a group not of one individual, and all present are
invited to join in the prayer for healing: *Spirit of the living
God, present with us now, enter you, body, mind and spirit,
and heal you of all that harms you.* On Wednesdays the evening
service is usually planned and led by guests, another way of being
drawn into the life of the community. On Thursday there is an
opportunity to make an act of personal commitment to Christian
discipleship, or to affirm a direction or renew a promise. Each
person wanting to do this joins others in front of the communion
table and then together with the whole congregation makes an
affirmation of faith. Friday is a time of farewell and celebration. In the evening there is an informal celebration of Holy
Communion.

A high point of each week is on Wednesdays when the community
conducts a pilgrimage around the island. At various stopping places
– the marble quarry, Columba's Bay, the Hermit's Cell, Dun I
(the highest point on the island) – there are readings, prayers,

stories – moments of reflection. Coming at the end of the summer season as we did, there was no Wednesday pilgrimage. Instead there was a walk to the bay where Columba first landed. It is a stony beach – some are rare translucent stones – and on a pilgrimage each person is invited to pick up a stone and to imagine it represents one thing in their lives that they want to be rid of. At the end of a time of reading and reflection the stone is cast back on the beach, and left there. There was no prayer or reading as part of our walk, but I picked up a stone nevertheless and said my own prayer. That stone I left behind; some others I still have.

The Abbey is able to accommodate forty guests, the newly-opened MacLeod centre fifty. There is also the Camus Centre of Mull – a stone-built salmon-fishing station, where young people come for adventure holidays.

The Abbey Community does not have much time to itself. The staff meets together on Friday mornings; there are staff lunches every Wednesday and Saturday and a staff social every Sunday night. Winter gives some respite from guests, and time to relax as part of the larger island community, an essential to maintaining good relationships. It also gives the community an opportunity for 'group building' – 'getting a good sense of ourselves before the onslaught'.

During the busy summer season the small resident community is reinforced by numbers of young volunteers; they come in groups of thirty to forty for six-week periods, up to a hundred in any one season. Each volunteer receives an allowance of £12 a week. They start work at 8 a.m., and may not get to bed until well after midnight. Twice a week there is a dance – a ceilidh – in the village hall. Singing, dancing, socialising, chores, prayers and talk are all an integral part of an Iona week.

'Well, what's the meaning of it all anyway?' Peter, a guest, threw the question out to those gathered in the common room after evening prayers. He was sceptical about a God who seemed impotent . . . to stop war and famine. One person was quick to provide some easy answers. The conversation that followed lasted until 2 a.m. Nine men and one woman stayed the pace. The next morning scrawled across the blackboard was a summary, 'We started out one fundie and eight liberals. We ended up all fundies and all liberals.'

'. . . people come week after week and find they are changed in some way'. Alison Newall experienced this herself when she came as a volunteer twelve years ago. It was the integration of work and worship that helped her 'to own' her own faith more.

It is like it was at Iona.

It is but a small isle, fashioned of a little sand, a few grasses salt with the spray of an ever-restless wave, a few rocks that wade in heather and upon whose brows the sea-wind weaves the yellow lichen. But since the remotest days sacrosanct men have bowed here in worship . . . From age to age, lowly hearts have never ceased to bring their burthen here . . . and here hope waits.

These words were written by a local historian, Fiona MacLeod, at the beginning of the twentieth century, when the Abbey was still an uninhabited ruin.

Fivefold Rule

WHERE the work of the community really happens is on the mainland or wherever its members live and work. The mainland work of the community is essentially what its members do. About half are in full-time ministry in parishes, chaplaincies and church organisations. Others include doctors, teachers, social workers, engineers, miners, a pharmacist, an architect, a librarian and a dairy herdsman. Some are students; some are unemployed. Many have been members all their adult life. Vows, however, are renewed on a yearly basis; members are free to leave at any time. Some may then become associates or friends; there are 800 associates and 3,000 friends.

Members commit themselves to a fivefold rule of life: to spend half an hour a day in prayer and Bible study, and to pray for each other daily using the community's prayer lectionary; to be accountable to each other for their use of money and also of time; to attend members' meetings (that includes meetings of local family groups); and to undertake to work for peace and justice, both locally and internationally.

This rule of life is one that has evolved over the years. It gives concrete expression to the community's three main concerns: work and a new economic order, peace and justice, and community and celebration.

The community first came into being at a time of widespread unemployment; it is living through another. In its contact with young people in particular it knows how many feel they have no value because they have no work. One of the community's planning groups is concerned with work and a new economic order, and looks for alternatives based on a life instead of a work ethic. A working group had been studying the implications of the new poll tax;[1] a tax that the community considers unjust and challenges. The working group put forward the suggestion that members who gain by the changeover to

the poll tax should put the difference into a fund to help those who are hit by it financially. On a regular basis members are encouraged to give away 10 per cent of their disposable income – 6 per cent to the local church or charitable concerns, 4 per cent to the community's needs and concerns. A small proportion of this, 3 per cent goes into a travel pool to enable all members to travel to community meetings without hardship. Accountability for use of time includes adequate time for recreation, physical activity and family time.

The early days of the community also spanned the war years. George MacLeod had fought as a captain in the First World War and been awarded the Military Cross and the Croix de Guerre for bravery, but later reflection on his war experiences turned him into a pacifist. Work for peace and reconciliation was a part of the community's aims from the beginning. The wording of the present peace and justice commitment, ratified in 1988, is a revision of that first made in 1966. It states that 'if we are true to the gospel of Jesus Christ, we must say *no* to the arms race and be prepared to disarm unilaterally.' Different ways by which members can engage in work for peace and justice include protest, study, non-violent demonstration, training in non-violence and political action for a more just world. By this is meant a redistribution of the world's resources in favour of the poor and hungry. The community also has a full-time justice and peace worker.

The community's concern for community and celebration is worked out in all the places where members live – in the inner city, on housing estates, in the suburbs and in rural areas. Whatever members have learnt about community and sharing is put to work out in the wider community to help counter isolation and loneliness, to build relationships and to encourage mutual sharing and support. The community's own 'family groups' are a support to members themselves. These are local or regional groups that come together on a monthly basis. Then there are the Columba Houses in both Scotland and England. Some who live in these houses are members; some are not, but all who do share the concerns of the community and support each other in their individual commitments.

The Peace and Justice Commitment
of the Iona Community

We believe:

• that the Gospel commands us to seek peace founded on justice and that costly reconciliation is at the heart of the Gospel.

• that work for justice, peace and an equitable society is a matter of extreme urgency.

• that God has given us partnership as stewards of creation and that we have a responsibility to live in a right relationship with the whole of God's creation.

• that, handled with integrity, creation can provide for the needs of all, but not for the greed which leads to injustice and inequality, and endangers life on earth.

• that everyone should have the quality and dignity of a full life that comes from adequate physical, social and political opportunity, without the oppression of hunger, injustice and fear.

• that social and political action leading to justice for all people and encouraged by prayer and discussion is a vital work of the Church at all levels.

• that the use or threatened use of nuclear and other weapons of mass destruction is theologically and morally indefensible and that opposition to their existence is an imperative of the Christian faith.

As members and family groups we will:

• engage in forms of political witness and action, prayerfully and thoughtfully, to promote just and peaceful social, political and economic structures.

• work for a British policy of renunciation of all weapons of mass destruction and for the encouragement of other nations, individually and collectively, to do the same.

• work for the establishment of the United Nations Organisation as the principal organ of international reconciliation and security in place of military alliances.

- support and promote research and education into non-violent ways of achieving justice, peace and a sustainable global society.
- work for reconciliation within and among nations by international sharing and exchange of experience and people, with particular concern for politically and economically oppressed nations.

Adult Muscles

THE Iona Community was fifty years old in 1988. The opening of the new MacLeod Centre marked this jubilee, its building an undertaking of faith commensurate with the earlier rebuilding programme. The new purpose-built centre replaces the old youth camp. It has been built with young people still in mind, but also to meet the needs of families and of the disabled. It has cost £1 million, a large amount of which has been raised in creative ways by members and supporters. A 'Go 90' campaign encouraged people to raise money by doing 'what they could do best'. People responded by knitting, painting, carving, dancing and even climbing mountains – for ninety hours.

A special jubilee edition of the community's newspaper, *The Coracle*, described the community as 'an early child of promise', that now has to 'flex adult muscles'. The fifty years had been only a 'beginning. The shape of the mission of the Church alongside the poor is changing – 1930s solutions will not do. There is much new learning to be done. The need for a supportive ecumenical network of people committed to radical spirituality and radical politics will grow, and it will require to operate within and out with the institutional Church.'

George MacLeod had his message, too, for the community. It ended:

'Again in our nuclear age, we have young people pledged to NON VIOLENCE: aware that it is the only alternative to this world's NON EXISTENCE.

'God has renewed his island – and now he is renewing us.'

CHAPTER SIX

Corrymeela

'HAS anyone here had experience of knowing how to handle their feelings about graffiti?'

'Is there something behind that question?' Ray's gentle probing response came from many years' experience of working with groups in Northern Ireland.

John, who had posed the question, explained that the problem was a new one in the town where he lived. The brightly daubed slogans that had now appeared near his home worried him; they could spark off the violence that is never far from the surface in Northern Ireland, even in the comparatively peaceful area where he lived. Perhaps there was something he should be doing about the situation. Should he try to remove the slogans himself? But then he had a wife and kids, there might be retaliation . . .

I was sitting in on one of the small sharing groups, members of the Corrymeela Community, and learning fast what being a member of this community means. John's question sparked off other members of the group, who told of similar incidents in their own neighbourhoods: of three women who had gone out at night with buckets of whitewash and removed slogans; of kerbstones that had been painted overnight in the Unionist colours red, white and blue. 'Then someone or maybe more than one person went out the next night and painted them grey again. The following morning they were red, white and blue again and this time whoever had done it had parked their cars over the kerbstones so no one could get at them. But one woman tried, crawling between the cars in an effort to paint them grey again.'

'I live out in the country,' the teller of this tale explained, mostly for my benefit. 'We've really had no trouble where I live, although our neighbourhood is made up of both Catholics and Protestants. Those who came in and painted the kerbstones in the first place were from the outside, but it's a way of stirring up trouble . . .'

Others listened intently as different members told of such incidents. After a while Trevor, who had sat silent up to this point, spoke up.

'What we have to bear in mind,' he said, 'is that our response to such incidents can be violent too. Removing the offending paint or graffiti can be as violent an act as the first. For instance, when I listen to that story of the kerbstones, it sounds to me like a case of which side is going to win. I think what we have to do is to find

ways of finding out who are the people involved and of getting into conversation with them . . .'

Which is pretty much what Corrymeela Community is all about.

Hill of Harmony

CORRYMEELA'S beginnings, however, go back to before the present troubles in Northern Ireland. In 1946 Ray Davey became Presbyterian Chaplain at Queen's University, Belfast. Faced with this new challenge, he thought about the years when he had been a field secretary with the YMCA in North Africa during World War II. That YMCA centre had been a marvellous ecumenical experience for Ray. It was used by Jews and Christians of many different denominations, and 'somehow it was so right'.

'I think that was in the back of my mind,' he told us, 'when I was thinking about this post at Queen's, and I decided I wouldn't call it a chaplaincy, I'd call it a community.'

What he had in mind was to give the students some experience of the corporate nature of the Christian life. He got hold of a house near the university and used that as a centre, and also took groups off to visit communities elsewhere: Agapé in Italy, Taizé in France and Iona in Scotland. It was also a way of helping

the students to experience something different from the sectarian type of Christianity that was only too common in Northern Ireland. These students were soon caught up in a ferment of new ideas – about the Church's place in the modern world, the position of the laity, the search for Christian unity and the growing interest in different forms of Christian community. It did not take long before the vision had emerged of a more permanent community somewhat along the lines of the Iona Community. The idea was shared more widely, and a group of about forty people – students and those older – began to meet together on a regular basis to talk and pray about such a possibility.

At a one-day retreat at the end of 1964 these ideas began to come together. A month later the group heard that a property on the Co. Antrim coast was for sale. It was owned by the Holiday Fellowship and had been used as a centre for open-air and hiking holidays. With the Iona model of community in mind – of both a dispersed community and a residential centre – moves were made to buy the property. These were successful. The name of the property was Corrymeela, a Gaelic word sometimes interpreted to mean 'the hill of harmony'. Given its appropriateness, the group not only retained the name for its centre but named the community after it as well.

'I am sure this is one of the great things God is saying to us as we gather here today. Have more faith in me, understand the sort of God I am. If you want a place where people can get together to know me better, a place where they can learn to think about my world and my purpose for it, a place where Christians can come together, especially those from different fragments of my broken body and learn to trust and love each other – if you want that – I want it infinitely more. O you of little faith.'

(Ray Davey, June 1965)

In October 1965 Pastor Tullio Vinay, founder of Agapé Youth Village in the Italian Alps, an international centre for discussion and encounter, officiated at the opening. Ray Davey spoke of his and others' hopes for the community: 'We hope that Corrymeela will come to be known as the "open village", open to all men and women of good will who are willing to meet each other, to learn from each other and to work together for the good of all.'

The Troubles

LINKS in those early days between Corrymeela and Iona were close, and still are today. The context is different but there are many similarities. It was emphasised many times during our visit that the centre is a resource to the community, not the other way around. It is primarily a lay community of 150 or so members, most of whom live in Northern Ireland. There are a few members in Dublin and some in England, mostly former members of the community who want to retain links with the community.

In the beginning all members of the community were Protestant, but its aim was to be ecumenical. Vatican II helped to make this a real possibility, and in 1969 the community truly became so with the addition of its first Catholic members. Little did they realise that this attempt to heal the divisions within the Christian community would gradually take them into the deeper waters of working for reconciliation in the secular community as well.

In 1965 when Corrymeela Community was founded, political leaders talked about the better relationships that existed between the two communities, Catholic and Protestant. In Northern Ireland Protestants outnumber Catholics two to one, and Protestants have wielded power since partition in 1921. The Protestant community's social and cultural links are historically with Britain, the Catholic community's with the Irish Republic. Religion and politics are inextricably linked in a situation where one community has experienced centuries of abuse from the other.

Whatever changes had taken place before 1966 to bring about a fairer sharing of power and resources, they had not been enough. In 1968 Catholics, angered about continued injustices, such as over the allocation of housing, founded – with some Protestant support – a civil rights association. Demonstrations gave rise to counter demonstrations. With the political instability that followed, the Unionist government requested the British troops to come in to help stabilise the situation. There are many views on the role of the army in Northern Ireland. Some said that it has prevented the situation from drifting into civil war, while others pointed to ways in which it has also increased the tension.

As the conflict in Northern Ireland escalated so the community's thrust towards reconciliation work became more central. The community found itself thrown into a whole series of crises which changed its shape and direction. Increasingly its members found themselves face to face with people, Protestants and Catholics, who were the victims of violence, and the community began to work with families and young people at risk. It began to develop programmes that aimed at a deeper understanding of the roots of violence and conflict within society, and in doing so members found they had to face these same roots within themselves.

The make-up of the community began to change. What had begun as a community of essentially middle-class people ('polite middle-class Protestants and Catholics') began to be more mixed,

not only denominationally but also socially. This, John Morrow (the current leader of the community) told us, brought about 'a melting pot situation that drove some people to run for the hills'. It meant having 'to think what difference there was for some of us between middle-class values and Christian values, and that was a terrifying debate for a lot of people.'

The debate is still there today. Chris and I were present when a discussion took place about the financial aspects of running the centre. It transpired that groups did not always pay the £1 booking fee if they had to cancel at the last minute.

'Why not?' asked a member.

'You must realise the reality of life in these parts. Money is very tight for many people.'

'Yes, I understand that, but £1 isn't much.'

'*It is,*' came the insistent response from another part of the hall.

Raw emotions had quickly surfaced. The matter was by-passed temporarily. But not for long. Another voice was raised.

'I'm not happy to leave the matter that way. We need to have a discussion some other time when we can take a deeper look at some of the issues involved here.' That was agreed.

Sharing Struggles

CHRIS and I were attending one of two members' weekends that take place annually at Ballycastle. There are other occasions when the community meets, usually five or six times a year in all. On these other occasions they are likely to meet at the Community House in Belfast or in one of the other towns where members live: Derry, Coleraine, Armagh, Newry, Dublin.

Membership of the community involves more than just coming together these five or six times a year. First, it involves commitment to Christ *and therefore* concrete commitment to some work of reconciliation. The words *and therefore* are written into the community's own description of what membership means, emphasising their understanding of what a Christian's responsibility is in a situation such as theirs. For some this commitment to a work of reconciliation is their daily job, for others it has to be a spare time activity. This may be expressed in their involvement in the classroom, youth club, neighbourhood or parish, or in peace education, the administration of justice or prison welfare.

Members also commit themselves to a personal discipline of Bible study and prayer. They can if they wish use the Daily Prayer Guide issued to all community members. There are Bible passages assigned for each day, and a daily prayer rota listing names of community members and areas of concern such as 'Christian unity', 'victims of conflict in other parts of the world' and 'other groups working for reconciliation in Ireland'. The rota means that all community members and members of staff are prayed for each month.

For support members also meet monthly in small cell groups, usually a group near where they live. Each cell group is responsible for organising its own programme; some include prayer, some are mostly social. These cell groups include full members and also Friends of Corrymeela. Some are specialised, concerned with working at understanding conflict or how to deal with relationships at work. One has as its particular focus prayer for Corrymeela and wider concerns. Then there are various sub-groups set up to help deal with the practical needs of the centre at Ballycastle or to help run one of its many programmes. One of these groups is the Corrymeela Singers, which travels widely not only in Northern Ireland but further afield, raising consciousness about the issues of reconciliation, and money and support for the work of the community.

Programmes are the events that take place both at Ballycastle and in Belfast. These are wide in scope, and set up in response to particular and changing needs. Prior to our visit to Ballycastle there had been a programme for adults exploring conflict and prejudice reduction; a reunion of young adults from Northern Ireland who had been on exchange visits with other young adults from Sweden and East Germany; a weekend for families with a member in prison; and another bringing together teenagers from West Belfast and members of churches from towns outside the city. All of these are situations that require sensitive handling and skill in group work. Members help to run these programmes, as do volunteers. Paid staff are likely to have professional skills, but all members are given opportunities to learn skills for themselves.

'Elementary skills which most people can learn to use in daily life,' John Morrow explained. This again means that members have to be prepared to learn about themselves first, to look at their own hurts and to share their own inner struggles. 'If you are not willing to do this yourself, you can't begin to help others. Yet we are very much a community of terribly ordinary people. All of us have our own very deep wounds. We are not a person's idea of an idyllic community. Now I don't find this discouraging; it helps us understand that we too are part of the problem of Northern Ireland.'

I asked him for an example. The one he gave was of a member not feeling valued by another and grumbling about that to all and sundry but never to the person concerned.

'We encourage people *not* to spread their disaffection by talking with others, but to try to share their feelings with the person with whom the difficulty lies – not accusing, but saying how they feel. We also ask those who find themselves "third persons" to encourage this process of going back to where the problem lies. Often there has been some total misunderstanding.'

John then spoke of how many of Ireland's problems are rooted in such misunderstandings and stereotyping of 'the other community'.

Being a member of the Corrymeela Community is demanding not only in time given, but in meeting such challenges. You are asked each year to consider seriously whether 'it is sensible for you to remain a member'. It is considered important for all members not to be so swamped with things to do for the community that they have no time for realistic involvement in their own situations. Those who decide to give up membership can ask to be Friends and thus maintain a relationship to the community. On average about ten members leave each year, and about the same number join.

Two Centres

THERE is constant coming and going between Ballycastle and Belfast 55 miles away. John Morrow lives in Belfast and we met him there at Corrymeela House. This is where most of the community's central administration is done. It is also a place to meet, a resource not only to the community itself, but to other groups working for peace and reconciliation. While we were in Belfast Billy Kane, Corrymeela's youth worker, took us to West Belfast, an area where Protestants and Catholics live in close proximity to each other in two housing developments separated by one street. On each side of the 'divide' Billy introduced us to a person well known in that community who then became our guide. He explained that it was not really safe for us to be in either area unless accompanied by some trusted person.

Either side there was little difference to be seen in the types of houses or the number of boarded up buildings; on the surface the only difference lay in the wording of the slogans painted on the huge murals that were a regular feature. In both places there was the strange feeling of being closed in; a physical fact, since there are actual walls and barricades to stop either community even seeing across to the other side. Introduced by a friend, we were greeted as friends and with the same Irish warmth, and perhaps most poignant of all, children on both sides crowded round Chris, demanding to have their photographs taken. Here both communities are poor economically. Joe, our Protestant friend, showed us some houses

that had been blocked up at one end because their backs were to 'the other side'.

'You tell them back in England they're "prody" houses,' he said, 'who'd like to live like that?'

It was not hard to feel the pain that is centuries old, and which runs through both communities.

A Prayer for all those involved in reconciliation:

> God, we believe that you have called us together to broaden our experience of you and of each other. We believe that we have been called to help in healing the many wounds of society and in reconciling people to each other and to God. Help us, as individuals or together, to work, in love, for peace, and never to lose heart. We commit ourselves to each other – in joy and sorrow. We commit ourselves to all who share our belief in reconciliation – to support and stand by them. We commit ourselves to the way of peace – in thought and deed. We commit ourselves to You – as our guide and friend.

The centre at Ballycastle is in a very different situation. The eight acre site on the Co. Antrim coast is right at the cliff edge. It is a place both awe-inspiring and blustery. Opposite is the island of Rathlin and beyond that in the far distance, Scotland. St Columba sailed past here on his way to Iona, a fact often shared. There is a complex

of buildings. One is a home for resident staff; three self-contained units can accommodate up to 120 guests.

One building in particular is at the heart of this complex. It is called the Croi (pronounced 'Cree'); the Irish word for 'heart'. Built partially underground, it gradually emerges from the hillside, its exposed walls of red basalt, quarried locally. Peace is its theme, a word engraved on the handle of the door at the entrance. Inside is a foyer and reception area with an open fireplace and a circle of easy chairs. A circular passage leads into the main part of this all-purpose worship and community centre. The building is like a heart, a womb, a foetus, an ear.

'It speaks differently to different people,' Michael Earle, the Centre's Director, told us.

In the room where we met daily for prayer a low table held a candle and an open Bible – symbols of the two traditions, Catholic and Protestant. In an adjoining room a large wall hanging depicts the tree of life that is written about in Revelation: 'the tree of life with its twelve kinds of fruit, yielding its fruit each month; and the leaves . . . for the healing of the nations' (Rev. 22: 2 RSV). The leaves for the Corrymeela tree of life were individually stitched by people of many different nationalities.

There have been discussions about the desirability of having the two centres so far removed from one another, and of having a residential centre removed from city deprivation and violence. But initially its situation is part of its attraction for many who come. Once there it is the kind of place in which it is easy to relax, to meet others, to sit and talk. And that has been important from the beginning.

'The central point about the ethos of the community is that it is very much about living, learning and sharing together,' John Morrow told us.

It was with this in mind that the idea of a residential centre emerged. Here Catholics and Protestants who have been conditioned to think of each other as 'the enemy', rub shoulders setting tables, washing up, tidying rooms. It makes it easier to then take the next step which is to sit down and talk. A lot of the programmes are kept that simple, providing a context for people 'just to have time to relax and share together'.

Other programmes are more specific and take the form of 'story-telling'. Participants sit in a circle and each is given the opportunity to talk about an aspect of his or her life. There may be questions and a discussion may follow, but the idea is not to have a debate. 'Debating doesn't really get you very far,' explained John. What does help is a person coming to a greater understanding of what has shaped him, or why she is that kind of person.

Anne told her story at the members' weekend. A Catholic, she lives opposite the Milltown cemetery in West Belfast where a gunman ran amok in March 1988 and shot into a crowd of mourners, killing several. She told us what had happened to her and to her family that day. At the end we all sat in shocked silence.

Later Ray Davey said, 'I live quite close to Anne, although in a very different area. To think that apart from Corrymeela I would never have known what had happened to her that day, and how she felt about it!'

Corrymeela also provides an opportunity for young people and adults to meet together for a more extended period of sharing and relationship building. Called Seed Groups, this programme brings together groups of young people over eighteen or adults over twenty-five, for four to six weekends spread over several months.

During one year over seven thousand people are likely to have visited the centre at Ballycastle. This is because it is able to accommodate at least three groups at a time. These include schools, youth clubs, unemployment workshops, families under stress, senior citizens, handicapped, clergy and interchurch groups, conferences for sixth formers and for adults on a broad spectrum of themes ranging from politics, faith and cultural traditions to Third World issues. There are also workcamps each summer, and a Summerfest when several hundred people come from all parts of Northern Ireland and from all over the world to join in a festival of sharing and exploration. Speakers at each Summerfest represent a wide range of nationalities and Christian traditions, and there is time to learn, to play and worship together.

Corrymeela could not sustain this busy programme without its team of volunteer helpers. The staff of about thirty includes ten long-term volunteers, who come for a year starting each September. In July and August short-term volunteers come for periods of one to three weeks and work alongside the long-term helpers in doing practical jobs and assisting with group work.

The new intake of volunteers were just beginning to settle in when Chris and I visited the centre. John, who had just started his year, accompanied us when we drove to Belfast. His first weeks had been great, he said. One of his reasons for wanting to be a volunteer for a year was to be involved with people; a change from books. He knew it would stretch him a lot and present him with many challenges. Already he was learning much that had been closed to him as a middle-class Protestant in Northern Ireland. He explained that at school he had only been taught English history; it was very one-sided. (Until recently it was mainly in Catholic schools that Irish history was taught.) Many more young people apply to be volunteers than can be accepted, and for some it is a first step to joining the community.

A New Thing

W HEN Chris and I arrived at Corrymeela there was a chaplain's conference for fifth formers from Lagan College in Belfast. Lagan College, one of the new integrated schools, is one of the signs of hope in Northern Ireland. There are many more. Members of the Corrymeela Community are quick to point out that they are only one group among many working for reconciliation, and there is a close working relationship between the groups.

About the future they are cautious. Members do not advocate any one political solution, although everyone had an opinion. That we learnt is not unusual. Recommending a recently published book at the members' weekend, a member quipped: 'The answers to the problems of Northern Ireland are on the blank page at the back!' Ray Davey, however, spoke of the different climate that is emerging.

'For the first time there is a very large body of people who want something different. It includes many people in the churches, a lot of communities and different groups and networks. That is a new thing; it has never happened before in Irish history. Maybe we are not being as effective as we might be, but we are here and we won't go away.'

CHAPTER SEVEN

L'Arche

H IS NAME he told me was Jean Vuaelin. He then told me the village he lived in, the name of his foyer (house), and that he worked in the gardens. He then leant close and told me he wanted to share 'something very important, deep from his heart'. Jean went on to tell me of the difficult time he had a few years back, how he had to leave the community for a while and return to psychiatric hospital, and how he had come back to L'Arche. It was at that time, he told me, that he started his job in the gardens; his particular job was delivering vegetables to the different houses. That suited him well; he was much better now and happy.

Jean is a member of the L'Arche community in Trosly-Breuil in France. He is a man with a mental handicap, and we sat next to each other at an agapé meal. Jean did not speak English, but another member of the community, an assistant, was at hand and translated for him. A little later in the meal Jean told me it was a special occasion for him to eat his meal with others. In his own foyer he usually ate apart, upstairs. It suited him better; otherwise he got too excited.

I was impressed by Jean's maturity; his understanding of himself and acceptance of his own needs.

'Yes,' Jean Vanier, the founder of L'Arche, commented later, 'it is the people with a handicap who are often the most mature members of the community. They are the ones who teach us.'

Language of the Heart

I T IS twenty-five years since Jean Vanier invited two young men with a mental handicap to come and live with him in a small house in Trosly. Their names were Raphael and Philip, not so severely handicapped that they needed to be hospitalised, but not able either to live outside without support. Jean wanted to provide a home for them and to help them integrate into the life of the village. What he experienced living with these two young men convinced Jean that here was a model of family or community that was greatly needed, and needed not only for the sake of the handicapped, but for the sake of people like himself, who could learn from the handicapped person a new language – the language of the heart.

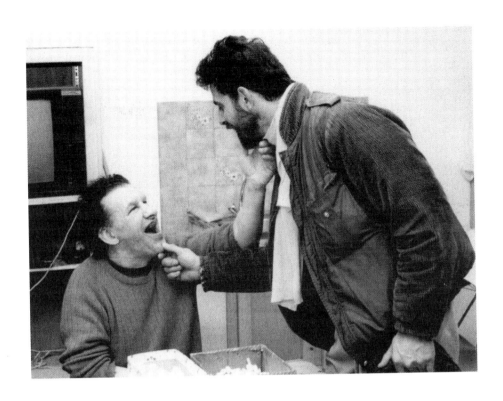

'We have developed in our Western culture a high intellectualism,' he told us. 'It tells us knowledge comes from concepts and ideas; we are frightened of the emotional and the affective. That is killing our hearts, and yet the fundamental cry of human beings is for communion with others. In our communities it is the men and women with a handicap who form community That is the mystery; the mystery that we will be healed by the poor.'

Jean Vanier speaks from his own experience; he gave up his job as a teacher of philosophy to found L'Arche, a family of communities that is now worldwide. He was encouraged and supported by a Roman Catholic priest, Father Thomas, chaplain at that time to Le Val Fleuri, a small institution for men with a mental handicap. They became co-founders of L'Arche. Father Thomas still lives in Trosly, and continues to give valuable counsel and direction to the community and its members.

Jean Vanier is himself a Roman Catholic, and at Trosly daily Mass is central to the community's day. As the community grew from one home to several and then expanded to surrounding villages, so Father Thomas saw the need for a 'house of prayer' that would be at the heart of the community. La Ferme became such a house and a twenty-four-hour prayer vigil is maintained here. Those who form the small community at La Ferme spend four to six hours a day in prayer in addition to their daily work.

It is also a place of welcome for retreatants and guests. Chris and I stayed here; other guests included several priests who had come on retreat.

In Trosly now there are six households formed of mentally handicapped men and women and assistants, and there are additional households in four surrounding villages. The handicapped men and women are referred to as 'the men and women'. 'How do you refer to yourselves,' I asked an assistant, 'if men and women is used for the handicapped'. Laughing she admitted that was a problem. 'Perhaps we are the third sex!' She went on to explain that the community wanted to find words that conveyed their respect for handicapped people. The assistants include numbers of young adults from all over the world who come for two to five years. Usually these are young people between the ages of nineteen and twenty-seven; some are older. Many have returned to their own countries and formed small communities there. In twenty-five years L'Arche has spread to twenty-one countries. There are now five communities in Britain, and in Europe communities in Belgium, Germany, Ireland, Italy, Spain and Switzerland. Outside Europe, the communities are widespread, in Australia, Brazil, Burkino Faso, Canada, Denmark, the Dominican Republic, Haiti, Honduras, India, the Ivory Coast, Mexico, the Philippines, the United States, and the West Bank of the Jordan.

Daily Programme

OUR second day at L'Arche Chris and I spent at the village of Cuise, five kilometres from Trosly. We were guests at Le Surgeon, a 'special needs' home for men and women who need constant assistance. We arrived at coffee time and joined the group sitting around informally, chatting, one of the assistants strumming a guitar. As usual the day had begun early at Le Surgeon; bathtime and breakfast take two hours.

At 10 a.m. the men and women leave to go to a workshop; here at Le Surgeon, however, there were two who attend only in the afternoons. They had been the last to be bathed, and lay or sat, warm and content, and spasmodically joined in the conversation, more by gesture than by words. David, one of the assistants, an American, told us he had discovered both himself and his faith in God at L'Arche. 'You arrive thinking you are going to give yourself unstintingly and then discover that is impossible.' He had discovered that he, like the men and women, had his limitations. He had also discovered strengths and gifts that he hadn't known about before.

At lunchtime we were joined by the others, assistants as well as the men and women. Some assistants may have work elsewhere in the community during the day, but everyone comes home for lunch. At mealtimes in particular, special assistance is needed. After lunch the men and women return to their workshop, and there is then some space for assistants to take time off, or there are tasks to do, food to buy, pills to collect. The men and women finish work at 5.30 p.m. Then there is the Eucharist for those who want to participate, or time to relax and unwind at home before supper. After supper there is usually an activity that assistants and residents join in together ('many celebrations') and the day ends with prayer. Each house has its small 'altar', a table with cross, Bible, a candle and some flowers.

The day is similar in all households. Each household, however, has its own orientation; some are big, others small; some more independent, others welcome the profoundly handicapped. There is Mass at La Ferme once a day; most members attend evening Mass.

At one Mass I sat behind an assistant accompanying one of the men, who suddenly and spontaneously in the middle of the service turned to the assistant and gently kissed him on his cheek. The assistant just as spontaneously and gently returned the kiss. It was a natural gesture of love, given and received, openly and without embarrassment.

The friendships formed at L'Arche between the men and women and the assistants are real and deep. Gabby O'Grady, who has spent

the past five years as a member of the community, told us she had come initially for only three months, but had been drawn back by the uncomplicated friendship of the men and women. She took us our first day on a conducted tour of the workshops. Great care was taken in each workshop we entered to explain the purpose of our visit to the men and women, and to ask if they minded if Chris took photographs of the workshop. A 'no' was always honoured, but most did not say 'no' for long.

The kind of work varies from the fairly repetitive – sorting screws and different parts for industrial firms – to the more skilled. In the craft workshops, the pottery vases, mugs and plaques, metal figures and sculptures are of high quality. Many of the designs and patterns come from the amazing ingenuity and imagination of the men and women themselves. They are sold in a small shop on the site.

At Trosly daily work also includes work in small teams maintaining gardens, or helping households with laundering and ironing or painting rooms. There is also a small market garden that grows vegetables, which are sold to local supermarkets and hospitals. The men and women earn a small wage from this daily work, in addition to the allowance from the government, part of which is paid to L'Arche for living expenses.

Support Systems

WHEN L'Arche began twenty-five years ago there were few if any models. 'We were very fragile,' Jean told us. It was this fragility, however, that taught them the need for support. At Trosly, L'Arche is given support by a board of directors, which includes among its members some professional people who give advice and counsel on administration and new developments. It also employs one psychiatrist and two psychologists (not members of the community), who are able to give advice, and are available for residents and assistants who want to talk to them. 'It is helpful for the men and women to have an objective person outside the community they can talk to,' Gabby told us.

Each community has its own board of directors. New communities serve a probationary period of five to six years. Each writes its own constitution, but all communities subscribe to a charter that lays down basic principles. Each has its director appointed for a two to three year period. Worldwide, L'Arche is divided into regions or zones each with its coordinator. The directors of communities in each area or zone meet on a regular basis. There is also an international council.

Each community is also 'accompanied' by two people, members of other L'Arche communities, who visit regularly and give objective assessment and support. Working in twos or in groups is an

important component of L'Arche's support system. In each foyer
assistants work as a team. 'That is very important,' Françoise
Cambier told us. 'Too much power invested in one person can mean
the most fragile people – the men and women – may get crushed.'

At Trosly some of the structures that have been there over the
past twenty-five years are changing. Françoise told us Jean Vanier
had been ill some years back, and that had shaken a lot of them and
made them realise they must plan for the time when the founder
was no longer with them. It was difficult, said Françoise; it meant
changing from putting one's trust in Jean as director to putting
that trust in the community itself. Jean has not been director for
ten years now, and the community is continuing to decentralise its
administration structures. There is a group of permanent members
that agrees policy and direction. Each village with its small group
of homes has its own 'responsible person', who holds that position
for three to four years, and is part of a Community Council.

For the first two years assistants receive pocket money as 'volunteers'. After that an assistant becomes salaried, receiving the
minimum wage laid down in France. There are, however, different
needs in the community. How to make the situation more equable is
a subject that comes up often, said Garry. Families had more needs
than single people. Some members put an amount regularly into a
common fund to help those with particular needs.

'Most of us who came here to Trosly early on came very young.
We are not so young now,' said Garry Webb. There are one or two
members who are retired. That is raising new questions for the
community: what kind of provision needs to be made for ageing
members. It is the kind of question that the board of directors is
there to help them think through. It has already arisen in relation
to the men and women. One house, La Petite Source, was formed as a
home for the elderly. However, several who moved there from foyers
deteriorated in health and died within the first years of its opening.
This seemed linked to the move from ordinary foyer life. Now the
elderly remain in the foyers, and are cared for there. 'Everyone likes
it like that,' said Gabby. 'The old people give so much; it is
like having grandparents around.'

There are at present 160 adult members. That does not include
children of the families. Some of these adults are the men and
women; indeed the majority, as we discovered when we arrived
for the agapé meal. This meal is for those who are fully committed
to L'Arche, and happens every two months. The men and women
are well able to make their own choices about membership and
to understand its implications, Christine McGrievy told us. Most
residents are referred to L'Arche by the social services, and then
spend two probationary periods in the community, a shorter and
a longer one, before a decision is reached about more permanent
residency. That, however, is not the same as membership of the

community. The deeper choice to 'live L'Arche and its values, to come to the point where one of the men or women will say L'Arche is my home, that choice is open to each individual'.

Choice applies to preferences about work too. Each of the men and women is given experience in different work areas, and if a preference for one or other area is indicated, that will be heeded if possible. Some may choose to move around, others to stay in

one place. It is a process that may take a while and sometimes the preferences stated are surprising. In the pottery workshop one of the men who works there stated clearly that was what he wanted to do. The assistants thought it was an unlikely choice, but they had been proved wrong.

The men and women are, as Jean Vanier said, among 'the most mature members'. 'The men and women know what they want. They know themselves, and they have a wealth of spirituality to share with others. It is the young assistants who come who have difficulty knowing what they want and making choices, who can't commit themselves and who are still searching.'

> Welcome is one of the signs that a community is alive. To invite others, whether strangers or visitors, to live with us is a sign that we aren't afraid, that we have a treasure of truth to share. If a community is closing its doors, that is a sign that hearts are closing as well.
> Love can never be static. A human heart is either progressing

or regressing. If it is not becoming more open, it is closing and withering spiritually. A community which refuses to welcome – whether through fear, weariness, insecurity, a desire to cling to comfort, or just because it is fed up with visitors – is dying spiritually.

But there is a time for everything: a time to be and a time to welcome. (Jean Vanier, *Community and Growth*)

Open to Growth

'THERE is so much that is impermanent in our society, so much that moves so fast so quickly. It is difficult for young people to know how and where to put down roots. This is also linked to the social and economic situation today. There is so much rupture and hurt. Young people who have never known any permanency or security in their lives find it impossible to commit themselves on a long-term basis to any organisation or to other people. Such commitment is essential for growth.'

Garry Webb spoke as Jean Vanier did about the needs of young adults today. He is one of a team responsible for welcoming guests and new assistants. What was involved in becoming an assistant, I asked. 'Life,' was the prompt and succinct answer. Garry then

elaborated. 'One's heart is involved; learning to become more vulnerable. Discovering somewhere in a deep way that each of us is called to be very real and very true. This comes from participating in a way of life which makes it possible for us to share deeply both the gifts and the hurts that we have received.' That took time he added; the length of time different for each person.

> I am more and more struck by the suffering of young people. It doesn't surprise me that some of them find it enormously difficult to commit themselves. Many of them have had more or less unhappy and unstable childhoods. Many have had very precocious sexual experiences, which can make later commitment more difficult. And then there is today's tendency to question everything. People are quick to challenge authority and anyone who tells them what to think. At the same time, there is the feeling that our world is changing with a terrible speed; everything is on the move. Young people can commit themselves for today – but tomorrow? We have to be very patient with young people who may in many ways lack inner structure and be incapable of giving a definite 'yes'. Their world is almost too existentialist. But if they find someone who is faithful to them, they will gradually discover what fidelity means and will be able then to commit themselves. (Jean Vanier, *Community and Growth*)

New assistants come first for a month's probationary period. The time may then be prolonged to a year if this seems right both for the person concerned, and for the community. A 'discernment group' is responsible for weighing this decision. After that year, an assistant may ask to stay longer. That is voted on in the community council. After that there is a period when membership can be renewed annually. For some membership eventually becomes permanent.

There are many different ways for members to participate in the life of the community. Some live out a call to celibacy. The assistants living in the households, sharing life with the men and women, are all single. There are also some single members who work in the community, and live in their own homes. This, however, is the exception. There are also families that are an essential part of the community. Some families have an attachment to a particular foyer. They share some meals and may have a resident to stay with them for a weekend. With the couples or families, either the wife or husband usually works in the community. 'How can I give the best of myself, and where?' is the question each person has to answer. Again, it is a question of knowing oneself.

> Community is made of the gentle concern that people show each other every day. It is made up of small gestures, of services and sacrifices which say 'I love you' and 'I'm happy

to be with you'. It is letting the other go in front of you, not trying to prove that you are right in a discussion; it is taking small burdens from the other. (Jean Vanier, *Community and Growth*)

Garry came from Canada to join the community fourteen years ago. He is a single man, who lives out a call to celibacy and is an assistant in one of the houses for the profoundly handicapped in Cuise. He spent his first nine years at L'Arche in a foyer, and then took a year's sabbatical. He then lived on his own for a while before returning to a foyer.

Children are also an integral part of the community. There were several children at the agapé meal we attended. Their relationships with the men and women are natural and uninhibited. One Canadian assistant we met had grown up close to a L'Arche community. Her parents had been closely associated with it. For her, too, it had been an important association. 'Most young people can't cope with those who are different from themselves in any way, people of another colour or race or who have a handicap. But I learnt early on to appreciate such differences, and not to be embarrassed or fearful of them.'

The mixture of single people and families is important to L'Arche, and so is the mixture of temporary and permanent members. It is not only a matter of having enough young adults to staff the homes, it is also a way of helping young adults to find a foundation for life. Each young person has a community member who 'accompanies' her or him, and all members are encouraged to have a spiritual director. These accompaniments are aids to personal growth. 'How do I continue to grow year after year? What is necessary?', is the vision that is held out to each member.

On arrival at La Ferme Chris and I sat down to a late night snack with a few of the community and guests. Into the room walked Claude, one of the 'men'. He took one look at Chris and went straight to him, admiring and stroking Chris's beard. My welcoming hand he viewed with some caution, and then turned away. He was gently admonished for his behaviour, but nevertheless stood his ground. He looked me up and down with indifference rather than hostility. That was all right. The last morning we shook hands, and I was glad of that too. There were other occasions when I, too, was made welcome by men and women with a handshake, a hug, an outstretched arm, a warm smile. It was after we had left and gone on our way, that I realised how captivated I had been by some of those I met; faces, strong and expressive, gestures of welcome or frustration, kept returning. For the men and women there are no masks, and with an uncanny knowledge they also see through and expose the masks of those of us who have them.

Sense of Belonging

'OTHER groups are called intellectually to community, but we are called through physical necessity,' Jean Vanier told us. 'Many communities are founded on mutual commitment, and that is often not enough. Our people cannot intellectualise, and so it is a revelation of something else. It is a community that is founded on fragile bodies that are crying out for friendship, and we should have died a thousand times if we hadn't been held by that cement.'

Jean widened the scope of what he was saying. 'I think Jesus is saying something to the whole Church through this. It is that community can only really function if its roots are the poor. Something happens to society when old people and the sick are not at the heart of the community, when they are abandoned by society. It is the weakest who are to be the ones most honoured.'

He continued: 'I believe we are at a particular moment in history when God is revealing himself through the smallest and the most fragile. We have reached a summit in the development of the intelligence, but it is not here that you find life. If you don't develop the heart, you develop the intelligence with flight from heart. What we are experiencing today is this incredible fear of relationship, and also the fear of those who are different from us. The pluralism in today's society makes people very fearful, but we have to learn to love the different.

'Our men and women are not able to develop the intelligence, and so they have developed the heart. Community is about belonging to each other, and it is in the heart that the sense of belonging grows.'

L'Arche Prayer

Father through Jesus, Our Lord and
our brother
We ask you to bless us.
Grant that L'Arche may be a
true home
Where the poor in spirit may find life.
Where those who suffer may
find hope.
Keep in your loving care all those
who come here.
Spirit of God, give us greatness of
heart
That we may welcome all those you
send to us.
Make us compassionate that we
may heal and bring peace.
Help us to see, to serve and to love.
O Lord, through the hands of your
little ones, bless us.
Through the eyes of those who are
rejected,
smile on us.
O Lord, grant freedom, fellowship
and unity to all men
and welcome all men into your
Kingdom. Amen.

CHAPTER EIGHT

A Base Community

AT EXACTLY 12 noon on the first Monday of every month, the siren sounds. It is a regular test by Holland's Ministry of Defence to make sure the siren works; this is the siren that would alert people in The Hague to the outbreak of war or nuclear attack. Each month at exactly 12 noon a small group of women and men put on white masks, pick up large white sheets and lie down on the pavement. The sheets cover their corpse-like motionless bodies. As the blare of the siren continues, two women move in and out, drawing chalk lines around the bodies. Passers-by move round or step over, disregarding the demonstrators as perhaps they disregard the piercing sound of the siren. Others stop, look, accept a leaflet that is handed to them. 'No Modernisation of Nuclear Weapons' is its message. Abruptly the siren stops, the bodies move, come alive again. The chalk lines remain, however, ghoulish reminders that such imprints of bodies are all that would remain if a nuclear bomb did indeed explode here. Among the demonstrators are some members of Ekklesia, a base community. Others are members of different peace groups, some from outside The Hague.

Hollanditis or 'Dutch disease' was a word coined in the early 1970s to describe Holland's peace movement. 'Help rid the world of nuclear weapons. Let it begin in the Netherlands,' was its slogan; its annual Peace Week brought together as many as a million people on to the streets of the capital to put pressure on the Dutch government not to accept cruise missiles on to Dutch soil. The Dutch churches helped to bring this about. In the 1960s they had helped to form opinion about human rights and aid to Third World countries; in the 1970s they turned their attention to the arms race. An Interchurch Peace Council was formed, and a large-scale educational programme undertaken. The response surprised even the organisers: Hollanditis had been born. A people who had lived through occupation, the Jewish Holocaust and the humiliation of its own Vietnam – Indonesia – wanted a different future for themselves and their children.

These movements for justice and peace had a further spin-off. Concerned people from many different churches, Catholic and Protestant, met each other for the first time. They attended the same meetings, worked together for a common cause, found themselves standing or sitting next to each other on demonstrations, and talked

to one another about their reasons for being there. Friendships were formed, some that often had more meaning than those in their own home congregations. 'What are we doing?' some began to ask after a while. 'We are together as Christians Monday to Friday, concerned about the same things, and on Sundays we separate and go our different ways. Wouldn't it make more sense if we were together on Sundays too?' Those who asked these questions were not just lay people, but included Catholic priests and Protestant pastors. In The Hague a priest suggested that a Sunday congregation be formed. He was part of a small group already meeting at St John's Chapel in The Hague. They sent out a letter inviting others to join them in forming a Sunday congregation, and the first official celebration of the Ekklesia Den Haag took place on March 10th, 1974, in one of The Hague's oldest churches, the Kloosterkerk. That became their meeting place until 1981.

Steps on the Way

'WE DIDN'T want to start a new church. In fact, I don't think we ever use that word to describe ourselves; a community, a congregation maybe, that is how we think of ourselves,' George Tanis, told us. Nevertheless, the name Ekklesia was chosen. Ekklesia is a Greek word from which the word 'church' is derived. There are other groups in Holland with the same name, mostly of students. These and similar groups are part of a wider movement of basic Christian communities in Holland and in other parts of Europe. The European movement also has connections with communities in Latin America, Asia and elsewhere in the world. In its beginning a predominantly Roman Catholic movement, it soon included many Protestants as well, and others who had no previous church connections.

It was in Third World countries that the base movement began and where it has grown fastest. In the early 1980s, an estimated 150,000 communities in Latin America alone. The word base is used to denote 'at the bottom of' society. In Third World countries the communities are comprised primarily of poor people; in Europe, certainly in Holland, members are mostly middle-class people, who try to be in solidarity with people at the base. Base is also used to mean 'of the people'. It is a lay movement, opposed to clericalism and hierarchy. It is also concerned with the *basics* of the Christian life, with simplicity and practicality.

In Holland, the base community is the 'most identifiable form of Christian community', we were told. Holland was one of the first European countries to form a National Federation of Basic Christian Communities, and to hold a National Congress, in 1979. There is now a European Collective of Basic Christian Communities, which is preparing to hold its Fourth Congress in Paris in 1991.

Joining Ekklesia was for most members the result of a process that had been taking place for some time. 'It started with me during the war,' said George Tanis. 'I was in the resistance movement, and I thought after the war we must have a different world. I was optimistic about this.' He found he was too optimistic. The fundamentalist Calvinist part of the Protestant church that he belonged to resisted his ideas. 'You came to feel you were an island in your own church,' said George. He and his wife then heard about Ekklesia; they attended one of the first meetings, and became members early on.

Gerrie van der Ven belonged to a reformed church, middle-class and traditional. An active member of the peace movement, she began to feel an outcast in her church. Hollanditis it seems did not catch on in all the Dutch churches. She found she had constantly to explain her activities to other members. It was wearing. She and her husband heard about Ekklesia and began to attend, but did not immediately become members. 'It is rather a big step from a traditional church to this [base] movement. It took us a bit of time,' said Gerrie.

Adrie van der Hoek moved to The Hague and looked for a church to join. She found one that seemed suitable, but soon came to dislike it. 'There were so many people, and I didn't get to know anyone. When you left church on Sunday, you didn't see anyone again for a whole week. People just sat there; it wasn't much of a celebration. The children didn't like it either. They just had to sit there and be quiet. They didn't understand what was said. I knew there had to be something else.' A friend told her she had been a member of 'a different kind of group' in another part of Holland. 'There must be something similar here in The Hague,' she told Adrie. They asked around and discovered Ekklesia. Adrie went, and found she 'really liked it'. At first she thought there was too much attention paid to politics, but came to see the importance of connecting faith with everyday life.

Jan-Willem van de Velde came 'to the point when I thought this can't be all there is to being a Christian'. Aad Sprut had been a Catholic priest. He had left the priesthood some years before he became one of the founding members of Ekklesia. At that time he was a pastoral worker with young people. 'The young people were not interested in what kind of denomination you belonged to. You either believed in God, or you didn't. That was the only distinction they recognised.' Bien Bottelier had been a nun for twenty-nine years, and then left her order. 'It was too cloistered.' She soon discovered she had the same problem with the church outside. Her dissatisfaction led her to Ekklesia.

People not Buildings

IN 1981 Ekklesia moved from the Kloosterkerk to its present home, the Bartkapel, a disused chapel in Schilderswyk, a poorer part of the city. The building seemed more suitable for a community which questioned affluence. At the Kloosterkerk 'everything was so very clean', George told us. As 'the oldest church in town', it was 'very stately, very beautiful'. It was a jolt to move to an old dilapidated building, and the move meant they lost a number of members, mostly those who had joined because they were disaffected with their churches, but who did not have the same commitment as others to justice and peace concerns. The move to Schilderswyk was a move in this more radical direction.

Ekklesia was told it could use part of the disused chapel, if it undertook to be responsible for its upkeep and repair. The other part of the building is used by a group called Emmaus. Their aims dovetail; Emmaus recycles clothing and furniture and runs a second-hand shop. Ekklesia upstairs stores Emmaus's recycled chairs; while storing them, they use them to sit on. 'One goes and another replaces it.' Members of Ekklesia like that; they keep their expenses to a minimum. 'We don't want to spend money on buildings or furniture,' Frans told me. 'People are more important. We attend to basic repairs, but we don't do more than that.' Nevertheless, the large room was full of colour and interest. There were wall paintings done by the children and young people, large posters reminiscent of various demonstrations, dominating all a large Cross: Jesus portrayed in the black figure of a Salvadorean peasant. The Cross was made for use in a public demonstration against oppression in El Salvador and is used each year in the annual celebration to remember the death of El Salvador's martyred bishop, Oscar Romero.

We seek the land

We seek the land where all
are welcomed equally
No one apart from their colour or race or creed.
No one apart from their colour or race or creed.

Near comes the time when we
all understand each other
Beckoning hands and opening all our eyes

Now here is heard the Voice
that had been silenced.
People are hoping the time of their freedom is come.
Here is the word of Her.
that makes us live on earth:
where is your sister, your brother who lives with you?

Here stands a table where
the way is shown to us
how we can live here as equals in trust and love.

(Text by Jan van Opbergen,
put to music by Jan-Willem van de Velde)

It is here that members meet each Sunday morning. When Sunday came Chris and I were given the option of walking or cycling to Schilderswyk. We were staying in another part of the city, hosted by Gea Boessenkool and Jan-Willem van de Velde. Neither Gea nor Jan-Willem own a car, preferring to cycle or use public transport. We said we would cycle, and were given bikes. There is not much traffic about on Sundays in The Hague; I was glad about that!

That morning the service was led by the young people of the community. For Chris and me they had prepared a greeting in English. They had also let it be known beforehand what they expected of the congregation, or rather did not expect. 'No applause please, just because we are young people. We are a group leading the service, no different from any other group.' Members of Ekklesia, including its younger members, are aware that oppression takes many subtle forms; ways by which one group or class asserts its dominance over the other

A different group is responsible for planning and leading the service each week. The organisation of this is simple; a list is stuck on the wall, and members form small groups and sign up. Sometimes they are *ad hoc* groups; at other times one of the women's groups or a theology group will take responsibility. Children and young people have their own programme, usually joining the adults for the last part of the service. Sometimes the gathering takes the form more of study or discussion than a service; if this happens, discussion will be followed by a song or two and the sharing of bread and wine. The sharing of bread and wine happens each Sunday. It is an integral part of the Sunday gathering, but there is no priestly prayer of consecration. One of the group responsible for the service will pray, giving thanks, and the bread and wine is then passed from member to member. In other base communities in Europe and elsewhere in the world, the practice varies; in some a priest still presides at the Eucharist.

Action and Analysis

JAN-WILLEM had cooked our first supper: a vegetarian meal. Chris was appreciative.

'Do you know what was in it?' asked Jan-Willem. Chris paused for a moment. 'Spaghetti, beanshoots, onions, green pepper . . . groundnuts.' 'Yes, yes,' said Jan-Willem, 'and do you know what herbs?' That was more difficult. '. . . oregano, thyme'. Chris was right. '. . . and cheese, a cheese topping,' added Jan-Willem.

Were all members of Ekklesia vegetarians? I asked. 'Not at all,' said Jan-Willem. 'There are those who say, "It is too difficult for us. It takes up too much time."' To help those interested get started, Jan-Willem has compiled a book of twenty simple recipes, with a suggested plan for progressing from meals with substitution for meat, to a completely vegetarian diet.

While some form of alternative life style is common to all Ekklesia members, forms vary, as do the activities that members pursue as justice and peace activists. George helped start and runs a 'World Shop', selling Third World products. Jan-Willem, a composer and musician, teaches mentally handicapped children to play musical instruments, one interest among many. Adrie is one of a number of women receiving social security who run a self-help group. Gea works part-time for the National Federation, combining this with feminist and peace concerns. Most members are active on several fronts – as members of trade unions, different political parties, national peace movements, Third World organisations, groups working with refugees or with the poor and marginalised in Holland itself.

The churches should walk in front at the emancipation of all groups of the population, including women. For the churches were founded on the words of the Jewish rabbi who, against the customs of his own day, met women as equals. He taught them the scriptures, which was not allowed. He accepted women as pupils and followers. He shared with them the mystery of his resurrection. He gave women the same rights as their husbands. And most radically Jesus liberates women from the stereotypes of wife and mother when he tells the parable of the lost coin: a woman who looks for a coin and finds God. (Maria de Groot)

Ekklesia does not set up its own organisations to meet needs it sees; its members look around to see what is already being done and add support to that. This is a principle all base communities adhere to. They seek to join together with all people of good will in working for a better world. A base community will only start a new action group if it comes across a need that is not already being met. Ekklesia is involved in one action like this. In partnership with a Protestant church in Schilderswyk (which means 'quarter of the painters'), it runs Food Line, providing low cost meals twice a week for people on minimum incomes. For all who come it is an important social event as well. Most arrive an hour or more before the meal is served, in order to sit and talk with friends. For some it is the only occasion in the week when they eat a meal with others. Other similar actions have been the setting up of support groups for Moroccan and Kurdish refugees.

Members of Ekklesia still meet each other during the week, sharing tasks or as members of other groups. '. . . and on Sunday you find the inspiration to continue . . .', said George. This is also when they share more about what they are doing, and learn from one another. The week we were there Adrie was involved in planning the next Sunday's service. Two of them were to share the 'sermon': Adrie to talk about her experiences as a single parent dependent on a social security allowance, and about the work of the women's self-help group. Another member who works 'on the other side of the counter', in the social security office, planned to talk about his work: 'How it is he does this job, and his concern to be as human as possible in the way he does it.' There has been collaboration between the two of them before – Adrie finding support for changes the self-help group were seeking. Sharing their work and interests in this way with other members at the Sunday service feeds prayer and concern, and also helps the community's analysis of what changes are needed both at a societal and a personal level.

As part of the wider base movement Ekklesia is concerned to move beyond charity to an analysis of the structures that keeps poor people poor, and to use that analysis to seek to bring about change. The analysis, however, is not just 'out there', but comes close to home in an analysis of their own choices, life style and attitudes. This is not something that one base community attempts wholly on its own; the national federation provides a place for broader discussion and joint action.

In the Lord's Prayer we say 'forgive us our debts, as we forgive our debtors . . .' Now what does it mean those debts? Do we apply it for example to the debts of Third World countries. 'I think it applies to that too,' said Jan-Willem. We were talking about different approaches to studying the Bible. The Bible is a prime resource in base communities, but is read carefully in its own historical Jewish context, with an eye to understanding its concrete application to today. The movement is wary of personalised or spiritualised interpretations that avoid its material or political implications. We went on to discuss the tradition in Jewish thought of the seventh year when all debts are cancelled, and to talk about Jesus's parable about the man whose large debt was cancelled, but who insisted on full payment from the poor man who owed him a little.

This kind of study is undertaken by the *ad hoc* Bible study groups and conclusions shared with the rest of the community when one group leads a service. In reading the Bible this way the community has been helped by the research and writings of a Dutch theologian, Maria de Groot, herself a founder-member of Ekklesia when living in The Hague. Other theologians who have had an influence are two Germans, Jurgen Moltmann and Dorothy Sollé.

As well as its 'theology groups', there are three women's groups. They are groups for sharing, support and building confidence. Adrie gave me an example of a group exercise she had found helpful. At one meeting she and other women with daughters

had written letters to them, recalling what life had been like for them as teenagers and sharing their hopes for their daughters' futures. The women had then read their letters to each other. In time, said Adrie, she would give her letter to her daughter, when older. The mix in the women's groups has sometimes raised tensions. In Gea's group, 'family talk' dominated for a while. They then came to the understanding that the first hour would be for such conversation, those who wanted something different came the second hour. Those in the women's groups also aim to spend time in one-to-one sharing; nurturing friendships is a priority.

We have the longest-winded breath
we are in need of the better future
to us belong the people who hurt most
the victims of the capital
with us someone already shared bread
that was sufficient for everyone.

We have the longest-winded breath
we build the human city
our allies are
the people without rights in the mental hospitals
the people without fields in the cities
with us belong the dead of the second world war
who finally want to eat justice
with us someone already rose
from death.

A quotation from Dorothy Sollé which is used often in Ekklesia and other base communities in Holland.

Members also meet in smaller groups once a month for a family meal. The group Gea is part of alternates a family meal, when all the children are present, with an evening meal for adults only. To plan meeting together more than this would be to counter Ekklesia's reason for existence. It is primarily a community of support for those who are engaged in work for justice and peace. Other spontaneous ways of supporting each other emerge. Gea and Jan-Willem are part of a small 'living-group' – more informal than a community household. Once a month Adrie's three children spend the weekend with this group. It gives Adrie some 'time for herself' on a regular basis.

The number of members has varied over the years, about sixty at the time of our visit. The difference between casual and actual members is the number paying a percentage of their salary to Ekklesia. Each member makes his or her own decision about actually how much, but a yardstick is about 3 per cent of earnings. The money is used to cover basic expenditures: heating and lighting

the chapel, administration, contributions to the national federation. The amount is kept low, since members also give financial support to other concerns.

'We are a community without hierarchy, with no fixed liturgy, looking outwards to the world.' How, I asked a group of members, did a community without hierarchy organise itself. There was immediate laughter. This had a history we learnt. At first there were pastors, who were responsible for the liturgy. After that co-ordinators were chosen to be responsible for the different sub-groups; in theory these groups in turn became responsible for the Sunday liturgy. Difficulties arose, however. There were Sundays when no group had signed up to be responsible. There is now an elected council who can keep an eye on this, and any other matters needing attention. Once a month there is a members' business meeting that is open to all. Chris and I were invited to attend and only a dozen or so members were present. The main item of business was a decision about Ekklesia's participation in a day conference organised by local churches on 'Justice, Peace and the Integrity of Creation'. The executive council had recommended not participating in this 'church event'; the members disagreed and voted to do so. People-power was still at work!

The parable of the excuses (Luke 14:12–24)
> To buy a field or five teams of oxen or to marry a woman these
> are economic values in the Bible. We find these values in this
> parable, but they are least of the values here. The people to
> whom the parable is told don't see this, or don't want to see
> it. We recognise ourselves in this parable. Those men and
> women to whom Jesus spoke saw a future opening up to
> them, but one they could only walk towards with open hands.
> To attend this feast would change their value systems. This
> is the most radical choice we can be confronted with: to open
> ourselves to God's future, and to let his future determine
> our lives personally and economically. (*Ekklesia, 1000 Dagen
> Experiment*)

A Modest Sign

IN THE immediate aftermath of Vatican II, there was hope that
the Catholic Church was itself moving in the direction the base
communities have taken. A vision of a Church made up of numbers
of basic Christian communities – of a parish as a community of
communities – was put forward by the Vatican Council. Now there
is an uneasy tension between Pope, Catholic hierarchy and the
base community movement. 'The people of God on the way' is a
description the base communities use of themselves. They have
turned their back on certainties, dogma, tradition – not in a heedless
way, but in a desire to be open to the new order God is wanting for
church and world. Another German theologian who is recognised as
helping to prepare the way is Dietrich Bonhoeffer, with his challenge
of a Christianity stripped of the trappings of religion.

Ekklesia's efforts are not directed at changing the Church as an
institution, but at working – as the people of God – for a fairer
and juster society. 'It is important,' Frans told me, 'that we do not
separate ourselves from the rest of the Church or from society. We
are not separate; we are part of both. But we want to keep a certain
distance too.' For this reason base communities take the position of
observers instead of active participants at the Netherlands Council
of Churches and its local branches.

An observer, but a modest one. Each year Ekklesia adopts a
different theme for reflection and action; the theme for 1989, 'Don't
try to have high ideals, but first look where you are, what you do
and what the outcome is'. There is a written constitution; one they
prefer to 'put in a drawer and shut it'. It is there to be referred to
if necessary. Part of it reads: '. . . following Jesus Messiah, striving
for justice and peace, we hope to be a member of the people of God
on their way . . . to become a sign of the messianic community in a
modest but still a real way.'

Our visit ended appropriately with our taking part in a second peace demonstration. This was a demo organised by the Franciscans, and took place outside the Houses of Parliament. We were each given a white cotton apron bearing a slogan: 'No Modernisation' or 'Don't build arms, build relationships'. Hollanditis has had its impact, part of the worldwide ripple effect that has helped to bring about some changes, but peace activists remain wary. 'No real dismantling has taken place yet,' I was told. 'Land-based missiles have been removed from some parts of Europe, but the number of nuclear warheads has not diminished; they have just been removed and put into sea and air missiles instead. At the same time NATO is talking about the modernisation of nuclear weapons.'

It was demo day in the square. Just behind us was a large group of Tamils and supporters, protesting against the deportation of Tamil refugees; beyond that a group bearing banners, 'No Military Aid to Turkey'. A decision the Dutch parliament was to vote on that day. In our group we had formed a large circle, hands linked. The person next to me spoke to me urgently in Dutch. I had to explain I was English and didn't understand. 'I think we don't have our backs to them,' he said. I understood. We moved apart to break the circle open to the Tamils behind us, to signify our support for their cause too.

Our group soon moved away. We formed a procession to walk from there to the Ministry of Defence. Gea and I walked together. We talked about the story in the Bible where the young David slays the giant Goliath with a small stone. 'I like that story,' Gea told me, 'of how David was weighed down with all that heavy armour and had to take it off before he could confront Goliath. It was as though he was saying, "I cannot fight for God with all this heavy armour on."' It is a story, too, that fits a community that has stripped itself of what it sees to be a lot of needless baggage in order to be the freer to fight God's cause.

CHAPTER NINE

Offensive Junger Christen (OJC)

'THESE days of shocking events and increasing unrest call us all to sit up and take notice. Those who point their fingers in accusation at this or that suspected instigator or saboteur should remember that the hand which points at others has three fingers that point to oneself . . . Doesn't that mean that we older ones have lost contact with the younger folks or have become unbelievable to them. Let us not lose the momentum for good that may come out of these turbulent days.'

Horst-Klaus Hofmann was one of many listening to these words of Gustav Heineman, then West Germany's Federal Minister for Justice, speaking on television. This was during the height of the student uprisings in Tokyo, California, Germany and Paris, that started in the summer of 1967 and continued through to the spring of 1968. Horst-Klaus was at that time general secretary of the YMCA in Mannheim. Daily in touch with young people who were part of or in sympathy with the student riots, he listened to their complaints about injustices in society and the dishonesty of politicians, and listened, too, to their fears and hopes about the future.

Then one morning as he was praying, he had an idea. Thoughts began to flow, one after another. He wrote down what he was thinking.

'Create and train a united, revolutionary team, a force to relate closely men to God, and effectively solve the burning problems of our modern world.

'Divisions in families, groups and nations; exploitation of emotions, conflicts and possessions; hunger, hate and hopelessness. The answer is, increasing involvement in the fight for the whole world.

'Whoever is committed to speak today to state governments, Church, and to management and labour, must be able to present a dedicated, intelligent and unselfish group of young people who take an active part in the modernising and salvation of our world.'

It was January 1st, 1968. He had asked God for guidance concerning his own future and that of his family. He felt that God had shown him what to do.

Revolution of Love

HOW TO start? The first step that Horst-Klaus took was to share what he was thinking with Mother Basilea, founder of the Evangelical Sisterhood of Mary in nearby Darmstadt. Together they decided to hold a conference for young people at Canaan, the home of the Mary Sisters. Invitations were sent out, and twice as many young people came as were expected. A second conference was held, and again numbers doubled.

The overall message of those early conferences was that being a Christian had to do both with personal life style and with a Christian's responsibility for society. Angela Ludwig, a member of the community, explained that at that time in Germany there were groups that emphasised either one or the other, but not many that spoke about the integration of personal faith and political involvement. 'Horst-Klaus would say that if you talk about peace you must know how to find peace in your personal relationships as well as seek ways to bring about peace in the wider context.'

Five or six conferences were held in 1968. It was after one of these conferences that two young women who did not know of each other wrote to Horst-Klaus and to his wife, Irmela, and both with the same request. They were trying, they wrote, to put into practice what they heard, but were finding it very hard. Could they come and live with the Hofmann family for a period of time in order to see how such a Christian life style was possible. Both added that they would be willing to help with the conferences and in other ways.

After some deliberation the Hofmanns decided to invite these two young women to become part of their family; they already had five children of their own. Other young people followed the first two, and the extended family grew to be 'the big family'. Soon the Hofmanns' house was too small. They sold it, and moved to a bigger house in Bensheim. By this time they had been joined by another couple, the

Klenks, who also opened their home to young people who wanted to come and live with them.

The move to Bensheim was important for other reasons too. By now Horst-Klaus had given up his job at the YMCA in Mannheim. The growing work took up all his time. The Mary Sisters home in Darmstadt had been a nurturing place, but there came the day when Mother Basilea told Horst-Klaus, 'You need to find your own way now. We can pray for each other, but we have different callings.' The Mary Sisters were very patient we were told, but it was not easy for them. Some of the young people who came to the conferences had long hair, smoked, whistled when the sisters went by, and climbed over the wall at night. Conferences continued to be held, but now they took place in centres in different parts of Germany.

The expanding work also needed a name. *Offensive Junger Christen* was eventually chosen; usually shortened to OJC. It is difficult to capture its meaning in English; *Young Christians on the Offensive* is too strident. Its choice springs from the different emphases that the early conferences were seeking to integrate. Angela recalled, 'The one group that emphasised personal faith were always trying to defend something; the other group who were concerned about politics were very aggressive. The name was an attempt to combine these two in a new way. We didn't want to be defensive or aggressive; we wanted to be *in* the offensive.' Her friend attempted some further clarification. 'Young people were talking about revolution; we were for a revolution of love.'

Head Work, Heart Work and Hand Work

'THERE is a wound in the soul of young Germans today. Twenty years ago they were ready and able and capable to work very hard. Today they are much more hurt and frustrated, and their answer is to build their own little private world.' Horst-Klaus was talking about the differences he sees in the young people who come to OJC today and those he and Irmela came to know twenty years ago.

Monika Wolf, another member of the community, also spoke about this. 'Today the young people who come are concerned about the future of the world, but they do not have the same willingness to sacrifice. There is a much bigger gap today between idealism and practice. It is a shock to many of the young people who come here when they realise how little they are prepared to give themselves unselfishly to others.' Angela saw another difference: 'Young adults today are much more concerned about religious questions; twenty years ago our concerns were more political.'

Twenty years have seen other changes too. The 'big family' has grown bigger still. The two families became seven, and by 1972 young adults were coming from many parts of the world to be part of this extended family. They came from the Philippines, from Mexico, from the United States and from other parts of Europe. A guest house was opened to accommodate the many guests who came for a few days or a week. Another development was the opening of a research centre, with an auditorium and library.

In 1979 Horst-Klaus had a phone call. 'Would you like to buy a castle?' he was asked. An old picturesque sixteenth-century castle in Reichelsheim 28 kilometres from Bensheim was for sale. The families considered this extraordinary proposition; it would, they realised, make a wonderful conference centre. One family decided to sell their bungalow and use the money as a down payment; two others added their surety to raising a bank loan.

The castle was bought. It had been used as a recreation centre for postal workers and was in need of major reconstruction work. That, however, was work the community was used to. Young adults had already helped with the reconstruction work on the 'Quellhaüs' and guest houses.

Chris and I stayed at the castle in Reichelsheim. It is a picture-postcard German castle with a chapel that dates back to the fourteenth century. The road to it is steep; few walk up it, though some cycle. From the top there is an expansive view over the valley, taking in the small town below. Tourists come daily in coaches and cars, and there is a coffee shop where they can buy food and drink and also find literature about the community and its work.

The young adults who join the community for a year, help run the conference centre at Reichelsheim. Some of the more permanent members of the community still live in Bensheim. In time, however, the plan is to move the whole community to Reichelsheim, still in a number of separate family dwellings, but all within an easier radius of each other.

OJC has grown larger, but extended family is still its ethos. Many of the questions that the young people who come to the community struggle with stem from a lack in their own family background, Irmela Hofmann said. Often this stemmed not from deprivation, but from a dependency that came from being given too much. This made them unable to form mature, adult relationships; many came perplexed about their failure to build consistent, loving relationships. On top of this they had to deal with the guilt of 'having everything' while there were those in other parts of the world who had nothing. Yet they knew they lacked the maturity to be able to do anything about the situation. Where do we find a solid basis for our lives? Who is going to answer our longing for a permanent change in our lives? Where can I learn to shape and share my life and to give it to others? These were the critical questions.

'At school we never discussed these things,' a young helper told me at one mealtime. 'I needed somewhere to go where I could talk about them, and where I could think about the direction of my own life too.'

What these young adults seek cannot be found solely in an academic institution, the OJC believes. What is needed is to provide an extended family context where they can learn responsible behaviour in the many aspects of everyday life. The programme the community offers is called 'a workshop for the future', and it teaches an integrated way of life, that includes 'head work, heart work and hand work'.

Clarity, courage and joy is what the community hope the young adults will take away with them. Clarity that comes from learning how to listen to God, courage that comes from studying the many examples in history or from the present day of people who have contributed to positive change. The extensive library at Bensheim offers examples enough; Wesley, Wilberforce, Drummond, Bonhoeffer,

---

The Beginning of our Revolution

Thank you, Lord Jesus Christ
Thank you that you called me and
accepted me in the first place
as a young Christian on the offensive
and that you want to equip me
and to make me effective.

Accept me, with all that I am
all that I was and all that I will be
I place myself at your disposal:
   'What do you want me to do Lord?'

So, from now on I will seek your guidance
and your will that I may act according
to your plan and your purpose.

Here is my life
   Myself with all my talents
   my friends and joys
   my preferences and wishes
   my time, energy and my money
   my fears and my hopes

I want to live for you and your purposes
and not for myself and my own plans
I want to learn also to suffer for you
and if it comes to it
to bear scorn
and to put my life at stake

Help me, here and now
as a young Christian on the offensive
to know what is the next step to take
and in obedience to take it.
   'May your will be done!'

Gandhi, Martin Luther King and Mother Teresa included. Joy that comes from a shared family life style where a day will often end with some shared festivity – music or drama or a birthday party. There are lots of birthday parties; each one is different and a major celebration. We saw evidence of one party: a large papier mâché bookworm hanging from the ceiling. 'She – the "birthday child" – is a passionate reader,' Angela explained. The day we left there was to be another celebration with dancing and music. Each meal starts and ends with a rousing song of thanksgiving.

The day begins at 6 a.m. There is then an hour of quiet; time for each person to pray, to read the Bible, to reflect on her or his own life and relationship to others. Everyone reads the same Bible passage as set in an ecumenical Bible-reading plan. From 7 to 7.30 a.m. there is half an hour of sharing in small groups. A person may share something from the time of quiet. 'In the silence you can get very uncomfortable thoughts,' a young woman explains. 'I always wanted to appear important and strong, never weak or as I really am. It was very hard at first to be open with others and say what I was afraid of, and that I was very difficult at times.'

Breakfast is at 7.30 a.m., and after that everybody (guests included) help with various household chores for an hour. That is followed three times a week by a further hour's Bible study; often the same passage as in the early morning, but this time the study is more academic. Theological questions are pursued, new possibilities opened up. There is then time before lunch for a couple of hours' practical work in the house or garden, or reconstruction work. The latter is never ending it seems. The community may be host to a group that has come to visit for the day, and at weekends to larger conferences.

Services are held in the chapel at noon each day and again at six in the evening. Practical manual or hand work continues throughout the afternoon. On Saturdays there is a particular tradition. It is open house at the 'Tannenhof' at Reichelsheim. People arrive early in the afternoon and meet each other over a cup of coffee. There is then a talk on an issue of topical interest, and after that tea together in family groups. Only it is not tea at all, but cocoa, and there are bread rolls with honey. It is the same every Saturday, and an almost unlimited supply of rolls as numbers are unpredictable.

I asked one young woman if she could tell me what the talk had been about. We arrived as it finished. She looked alarmed; her English did not run to that, but she shared the one thing she had found particularly helpful. That was the suggestion that each person needed to find one radical issue to take up that was important for him/her. 'I needed to hear that,' she said, 'I get confused with so much that needs to be done.'

While they are at OJC the young people are challenged to consider their responsibility for God's world. The community itself supports

different development projects in Asia, Africa and Latin America. Every Christmas it sends out a letter to friends and supporters describing these projects and asking for contributions, and at the same time urging them not to spend so much on Christmas gifts but instead to give sacrificially to those in need in other parts of the world.

OJC, however, is careful not to align itself with any one political party or campaigning group, although it may support a particular campaign. It flew a balloon from the castle tower as part of a successful campaign to stop military planes from a nearby air base endangering lives and property by low flying. The planes still fly over, but higher. While encouraging young people to become involved socially and politically, the community also cautions them not to get into polarised positions where they consider theirs is the only right way.

While we were there the community was in the process of buying a farm near Reichelsheim, and had started an ecological institute. Ralf Glahs had recently come to join the community following two years' training as a horticulturalist. He had already established an organic garden at Bensheim, and was looking forward to working as part of the farm at Reichelsheim.

Renewing from Within

THE majority of those who come to OJC do so for one or two years, but there are several who have been in the community for fifteen or more years. Nevertheless, it is only within the last five years that the community has begun to think about permanency of membership. A number have now stated their intention to stay in the community for the rest of their lives – 'unless anything drastic happens'. That means the community is thinking about the obligations of permanent membership, and also the possibility of some kind of associate membership for those who come and then leave.

The Klenks – Hermann and his wife, Friederike – were the second couple to join the Hofmanns. Hermann gave up his profession as an architect to help Horst-Klaus and Irmela in the work with young people. It was not an easy decision for him, but one that he felt was right. Being an architect he told me is 'in his bones'. Part of what God has taught him over the years is to change his priority from buildings to people; there has, however, been plenty of scope for both in recent years. That was something Hermann did not expect in the beginning. Then there were no prospects of his being able to use his professional gifts as part of the growing work. That changed early on. The 'Quellhouse' and the guest house were old houses that needed a lot of reconstruction work. Later came the castle and the skeleton of its old Gothic chapel. This work provided plenty of hand work for young adults, and rebuilding old houses also fitted well with the community's philosophy of building. 'We like to take old houses and rebuild them, not build new ones. It is the same as with people; we hope that God is renewing them from inside.'

Both at Bensheim and at Reichelsheim the houses are spacious, yet welcoming, and everywhere there are paintings and ornaments that harmonise and also intrigue. Statues, sculptures and woven tapestries are from many parts of the world, from Africa, Asia and Latin America. An appreciation of art and culture is part of what the community wants to encourage. It decries the break between culture and faith that has too often happened with pietistic groups.

In the room where I slept a water colour painting hung over my bed. It was very simple; two windswept trees on a green sward. It was however so striking that I asked Michael Wolf, the conference centre's director, who had painted it. There were I noticed many similar water colours in other rooms and along passageways. It was he told me the work of a well-known German painter, Rigo Schmitt. Rigo Schmitt died in 1988. He had spent his last years at Reichelsheim, nursed by the Wolfs. The water colours he had painted for the community during those last years. In the chapel at Reichelsheim a large oil painting stands at the back unfinished; it is also the work of Rigo Schmitt.

For the last thirteen years the practical side of the reconstruction work has been the responsibility of Dierk Hein. He and Hermann Klenk work closely together; 'he has the ideas, I can do them'. Dierk learnt the building trade early on as a seven-year-old boy helping his father to rebuild an old farmhouse. Later at university he trained to be both a mechanical and an electrical engineer. He was then offered a job lecturing in the university, and he and his wife, Ursula, formed a small community with two other couples. The couples did not stay together long, but the Heins' continuing desire to live in community brought them into contact with OJC. They joined in 1976, and Dierk began to use his building and engineering skills within the community. He encountered similar difficulties to Hermann Klenk. 'I just saw the things to do; I didn't see the people.'

These were unskilled young people who had come to the community to learn how to live. Dierk realised he had a lot to learn himself. One of the unwritten obligations of being a community member is to learn how to love others. There are others: to depend first on God not on people; to be willing to do whatever needs to be done, and to trust the others in the community.

The more permanent community members ('the team') meet together once a week, and once a month there is a meeting of the whole community, short-term members included. Once a year the team takes a three-week retreat together, away from home. 'Plenty of time to take walks together, to share, to talk over any difficulties

we are encountering, to put right any differences.' Not that any
soured relationships are left to fester until the yearly retreat;
openness with each other is what is expected, and sometimes
such matters are broached through a written note or letter. 'We
find that for many people that is the best way; it is easier for them
to express themselves in writing.'

Such openness in relationships is not easily learnt. Cornelia
Geister told us she began to learn how to do this in the early
morning times of sharing. The first hour on her own spent in Bible
reading, prayer and reflection had helped her to become more sure
of herself as someone with her own identity apart from parents and
friends. The opportunity then to share with others what she was
learning about God and about herself had taught her confidence
and the ability to be open with others. These times of early morning
sharing are carefully structured; they are not times for correcting
others or for commenting on what another shares, but for careful
and receptive listening.

Cornelia has been in the community seventeen years; she was
among the first group of young people who came to live with the
Hofmanns. At that time she did not know what she wanted to do
with her life, except at times to feel like ending it. Her relationship
with her father was difficult, and her belief in God non-existent.
She saw in the Hofmanns and their family the hope that life
could be different for her. As it has become. She took a training
in publishing, and she now works in OJC's publishing department,
editing the community's bimonthly newsletter (sent free of charge
to friends all over the world), and its many magazines and books.

Angela Ludwig likewise came to the community as 'someone
who didn't believe in God', but felt drawn by its atmosphere of
openness and love. 'You don't need to believe in God, but you do
need to come open to the possibility that he exists and can speak
to you,' Irmela Hofmann told her. Angela had been a member of
a community before, a small community of Marxist students, but
it had not been a good experience for her. It made her nervous of
joining another community, but two years living as a part of the
Hofmanns' extended family helped her to find both a relationship
to God and the kind of balance she had been looking for in her life.
'Everything was in my head before,' she told me. Not only that,
but she had a broken relationship with her own parents, and an
inability she had found to sustain other kinds of relationships. She
and Cornelia are well able to empathise with the young people who
continue to come year after year to OJC, many with very similar
experiences.

The Coming Generation

OJC IS an evangelical community; 'pietistic' is the word it uses. Its brand of pietism is however different to most. 'We don't believe in separating pietism from daily life, or personal faith from social and political involvement'; this phrase or similar was repeated many times.

It is a community that believes in God's intervention in daily life and his ability to supply its material as well as other needs. We saw the reconstruction crew working on a new office building in Reichelsheim. The building had been bought for them by a friend. We heard, too, of another friend who had sold a flat she had been keeping for her retirement and given the proceeds to the community. It had been an unexpected gift. Not long before she had rung Horst-Klaus, introduced herself and said, 'I'm interested in your work, but I've been warned that you mix politics with religion. Is that true?' 'Come and see what we do,' Horst-Klaus had replied. She had, and the gift had followed.

Dierk Hein had another similar story. Some time before, he, too, had a phone call. 'I build staircases,' the caller had told him. 'Do you want me to build one for you?' At that time the community had no need of his skills, but now they had. A staircase was needed for the new office building. 'It's the electronics of the Holy Spirit,' said Dierk.

Community members receive 200 marks a month, families an additional 100 marks for each child. Those who come for one year receive 50 marks a month. 'We want to learn to live simply,' said Cornelia. She added, 'But you know each of us receives a lot of personal gifts from families and friends. It is hard to say that we live that simply.'

It is also a community that draws theologically from many sources, from the evangelical or pietistic to the more catholic and also liberal. The books that line the shelves of Horst-Klaus's study bear witness to this. A large section is of books by John Stott, an 'elder statesman' of British evangelicals, who like Horst-Klaus is concerned about the integration of faith and daily life. There are also books by an Argentinian theologian, René Padilla, a close friend of the community's, and by a number of German theologians, including Karl Barth, Emil Brunner, Paul Schütz, Adolf Schlatter, Karl Heim and Klaus Bookmuehl.

Dietrich Bonhoeffer has been another important influence. Before we left, Horst-Klaus photocopied for me a passage from one of Bonhoeffer's writings. In it there is a sentence that he quotes often.

'The ultimate question for a responsible man to ask is . . . how the coming generation is to live.'

CHAPTER TEN

St Egidio

'**E**ACH of us takes part, in living in the desert of the city, in a twofold struggle: on the one side against the injustices of human society, on the other against our old attitudes.'

(Orientations for Our Common Life)

'That's when I discovered the poor of Rome, when I was in . . .' Monica's next words were lost to me. She was shouting above the noise of the traffic; a blaring, honking constant sound that is particular to Rome as to nowhere else. When there was a lull she repeated what she had said.

'It was when I was in high school. Some members of the Community of St Egidio came to our school to talk about their work. I wasn't much interested in what they said or in what they did, but I was interested in them. I had never met people quite like them before. Some of them became my friends, and of course they said, "Come and see what we do." It was then that I discovered the poor of Rome.'

It was not long before Monica became a member of the Community of St Egidio herself. She is still a member, ten years later, and expects to remain so for some time to come, possibly for the rest of her life. She shares a flat with four other women, and each day revolves around serving the poor of their city. Other things are fitted in around that.

Monica had just completed her graduate studies the week before our visit to the community, and had started a part-time job doing research for the city council into Third World immigration problems in Italy. Most members try to find jobs that bring them into such contact with social needs, and most only take part-time jobs, in order to be able to give the other part of their time to voluntary work in one or more of the community's services. That takes up more than just the rest of the working day, as we were soon to discover.

Monica's parents' concern about her decision to become a member was perhaps understandable. 'At first they worried, but this was mostly because they thought it would interfere with my studies. When they realised it was possible to do both, they stopped worrying.' Those whom Monica met in the first place had not been long out of high school themselves. It was in a high school too that the Community of St Egidio began. Only it was not called that then.

Discovering the Poor

FEBRUARY 7th, 1968 was the birthday of the community, and this day is still celebrated as such. Now, however, the community has so many members and is so widespread that it is not possible for them all to celebrate the birthday together in one place at the same time. 'How many of you are there?' I asked Monica, not long after our arrival. The standard question. This time it was met with a long silence. Then, 'Well, you know, that is not so important to us . . .' Nevertheless, I pressed her. 'Oh, maybe, in Rome itself, three thousand. Outside, two thousand perhaps.' I looked at her astonished, and presumed I had heard aright. I had, but in the beginning it was only a handful of high school students. Later I was to discover that the actual number of members is more like three times Monica's embarrassed figures.

Mario Marazziti, another of our hosts, told us in halting English what actually happened on February 7th, 1968. 'Some high school students, some with a religious background, and some without, started to have a small meeting together once a week, from the necessity to create something different from loneliness, *something hot*. That first meeting was about loneliness, for the normal experience was to be many together, without being together, and everyone was looking for something more involving. The choice was made to go on meeting together, and to start looking at the gospel, because they didn't know it very well, and trying to read it in a very simple way. The decision was if there are things written in the gospel that it says we have to do, let's try and do them . . .'

What had stirred them initially, Mario told us, were the student protests of that year and the year before, 1967 and 1968, that had broken out in many countries, including Italy. The high school students' concern was to find a way to live seriously in the face of the world's many problems. In the gospels they read that Jesus was concerned with the needs of poor people. Were there, they wondered, many poor people in Rome? The school they belonged to was the prestigious Virgil Lyceum High School; all the young men came from well-to-do middle-class families. They had never really considered this question about poor people before. They did not have to look far to discover their answer. Outside the centre of the city, on the banks of the Tiber, they found a shanty town similar to that in Third World countries, with up to 100,000 emigrants from Southern Italy living in corrugated iron shacks. In addition, they discovered another 600,000 or so poor people living in an area near by, the 'borgate'. These people were poorly housed, with inadequate health care and educational facilities.

What could a handful of high school students do? They did what they felt they could do best. They started a Scuola Populare (School of the People), and began to teach Sicilian children how to read and write. Now they were almost daily in and out of these neighbourhoods. They learnt people's names, listened to their stories and began to understand something about the human and social problems that lay behind the appalling circumstances they now encountered. Perhaps because of students' age, the oldest was only eighteen years and one month when the community first met, they did not have any ready-made answers. One thing they knew they could offer was friendship. This meant finding a way to build relationships with people very different from themselves, and discovering they were confronted daily with their own prejudices and with the need to be absolutely honest about their motives for offering friendship and practical help. Their motivation was to follow the example of Jesus himself, who was a friend to the poor of his day. These early experiences have formed the community into what it is today.

Its aims are prayer, fraternity and service of the poor. The community seeks to give practical help wherever it sees a need. It also works for change at the political level, but does not support any one political party. The starting place is always the personal: meeting people as individuals, valuing them and building relationships. To be a friend, to pray, to serve others is something everyone can do, explained Mario. Even if you are poor, it is something you can do. In this way a community has been built up that includes not only young people, but old as well, not only the highly educated, but also the uneducated and illiterate.

> The large modern city poses new and grave problems both for societal life and for the Church. Its huge dimensions, its structural unfriendliness, its sprawling peripheral areas (both in the urban and in the human sense), make the city into a difficult place to live, with little sense of community, where the individual, even in the midst of a crowd, is isolated and unable to become part of a shared human life. Poverty and dramatic events form part of the day-to-day experience of each one of us. Our own community, with the sensitivity born of the reading of Scripture, is aware that the city is like a desert, despite its multitude of inhabitants.
>
> The monastic fathers abandoned the city in order to serve the Lord with complete freedom. For Anthony, the retreat into the desert was the beginning of the formation of a community of monks which surrounded his experience of searching for God. Benedict, too – according to St Gregory – left the city and retired to the solitude of the countryside to establish a monastic family. Today the place of testing for whoever would find God would seem no longer to be outside the city,

but in the immense desert of urban loneliness. This is the true desert of the search for God, where the disciple, like his Master, must fight against the triple temptation with the aid of the Word of God, just like Our Lord did in the desert, when faced with the temptations of the Devil. (*Orientations for Our Common Life*)

Their Dream

'THE Community' they called themselves when it was only a small group meeting a Virgil Lyceum High School. Soon, however, they were looking for others to join them, and started to share the dream they had with other high school students, girls as well as boys. The dream, a word used often by those we met, was not only of service to the poor, but also of community. They had read together the passages in the New Testament which tell how the first Christians met together daily to pray and to be instructed in the faith, and how they sold their possessions and put the money into a common fund to provide for those in need. They too wanted to be Christians who met together daily to pray, to study the Bible and who met the practical needs of those around them. Soon it was the community at Virgil Lyceum School *and* the community of Mamiani School, *and* the community of Primavalle neighbourhood, for when they shared their dream with their new friends out in these neighbourhoods, they also wanted to be part of it. In this way the community grew both in the centre of Rome, and on its outskirts.

Most of the students were members of the Roman Catholic Church, and so the community was 'kind of Catholic'. The founding group left the Virgil Lyceum School, and went on to further studies or took jobs. They continued, however, to meet daily, and to work among the poor. Many of their elders, including priests to whom they talked about their dream, were sceptical. 'When you grow up, it will disappear and what you have started will finish,' they said.

Attitudes, however, were changing gradually in the Catholic Church; Vatican II had itself talked of 'discovering Christ in the face of the poor', and of the need to encourage and support lay movements in the Church, movements 'from below', 'of the people'. 'The Community' was certainly such a movement. In the early 1970s one priest asked to become part of the community, not to 'impose himself on it, but because he loved what was happening'. He was given permission to do so, and that was the beginning of a change in the community's relationship to the official Church. It also paved the way for its getting permission to use a disused church, the church of St Egidio with its adjacent ex-monastery, as

premises. From this point the community took the name of St Egidio (St Giles in English) as its own.

Now those who lived in the centre of Rome had a place where they could all meet together daily. Every evening at 8.30 p.m. the church is open, and people come to pray. Not all are able to come every evening, but always there are around 150 who do. The church, in fact, is not big enough now to contain all the members at one time, but every day other churches are similarly open mid-evening and members come together in three sub-groupings. In addition to the services in St Egidio, we attended a service in the ancient basilica of St Maria in Trastevere; 200 or more were there. Three other services were being held elsewhere at the same time.

That the churches are open at this time in the evening is significant in itself, for by this time all others in Rome are closed to visitors. This is a time when visitors to Rome are still idling their ways through Rome's many squares and back streets, and an open door is inviting. A number of the community's present members and

supporters have come to know of them this way, drawn first by their curiosity to discover what such a young congregation could be doing at such an hour. In just such a casual way further communities elsewhere have been born. In twenty-one years the community of St Egidio has grown to include groups in Naples and other cities of Italy, in Belgium and Germany, and in other countries. While we were there, young people had come from Mexico, Mozambique and the Ivory Coast to spend a period in the community prior to forming one of their own back home.

Gift of Friendship

THE community's gift of friendship is unique. I was to discover this on more than one occasion.

Clutching a paper bag, his grey hair long and uncombed, Marcello asked, 'And what about your Mrs Thatcher?' Paulo, one arm affectionately around his friend, had introduced us. 'Here is a friend of mine who speaks perfect English,' he told me. Marcello did indeed speak perfect English; in fact he spoke five languages. Articulate, informed, he asked me about what Mrs Thatcher was doing to our health service, and what was this about a poll tax? 'Why do you allow her to do these things?' he wanted to know. We went on to talk about why the rich get richer and the poor get poorer, not only in Britain, but in Italy and all over Europe. Marcello was speaking from his own experience. He had been a tourist guide in Rome, on contract to a large firm. The firm had not paid his insurance stamps, so he had no pension. Now he was homeless and penniless and came every day to the soup kitchen run by the community. The community were also helping him to take up the matter of his pension with the authorities. 'But here in Italy the system is very slow . . .'

Outside the door of the soup kitchen, that day's menu is written up. Mario comes to Chris and asks, 'What is this?' In his hand he has a small white pea. 'A chick pea,' Chris tells him. Mario laughs, and makes a change to the menu. It had said chicken instead of chick peas. That had caused trouble! The menu is written in English as many who come are foreigners who know English but no Italian. At this soup kitchen the community serves on average seven hundred every evening; the food is provided for the most part by the city council. One room is for foreigners, the other for Romans. The community may consider both their friends, but not all who come have the same attitude.

I had come to help. 'Work her hard,' Mario had said laughing, as he left me there. There was no problem about that. This was no self-service cafeteria-type soup kitchen, but one where those who come are served. I had to serve two tables; all five courses are served separately: a pasta dish or soup, a main dish of meat and veg, cake, fruit, coffee. Bread rolls and fruit are piled up in wicker baskets, and served not with your hands but with tongs. Many asked for several rolls and pieces of fruit. That would be their breakfast tomorrow. While I served two tables, other community members were there to sit and talk with those who came, and came not only for the food, but for the conversation and friendship, too.

Angela was complaining to Stefan. He had to translate for me. 'She says she wants something to warm her inside.' 'Doesn't my friendship with you warm you?' he had asked her. 'Yes,' Angela had replied, 'but only when I am in here. Soon I shall be away again.' When Angela heard I was a writer, she told me her father was, too. 'Indeed,' Stefan told me, 'many of these people come from well-to-do families. There are many reasons why they have fallen on hard times, but some of them have lived this way now for twenty years or more.'

I worked for two hours non-stop. At 8.30 p.m. Monica came to fetch me. I was to go with her and other members of the community to the Termini Central Station in Rome. Every Tuesday evening they do this, taking with them large bags of rolls and flasks of soup. The rolls are prepared by women and elderly people in the neighbourhood communities on the outskirts. 'See they fill them full of good things that give energy.' Indeed, the rolls were bursting with good things, each in its own plastic wrapping. Which was as well, for many of them were put by for tomorrow by those who took them.

'You are a little late tonight,' Pietro told us. On our way Francesca had explained, 'Many of them know it is Tuesday because that is the evening we come.' Here, too, they know everyone by name. A woman ambles up to us, unsmiling. 'What is wrong?' asks Francesca. 'It is as usual,' came the reply. 'No, something is wrong,' insists Francesca. The woman gives a sad shake of her head, but will not tell. Francesca goes off to find Roberto. He is this woman's particular friend, she explains to me. Roberto finds out that a close friend has died; she would like to go to the funeral, will he go with her? 'He will go with her,' Francesca tells me, 'we are the only people they can ask to help in such ways.'

Inside the station we come across Carmel, dirty, her stomach swollen, her legs likewise swollen and bandaged. She is curled up uncomfortably on a board. Francesca talks for a while, but then tells her sharply, 'You must go to the hospital'. Carmel looks alarmed. She is afraid of enclosed places. Francesca cannot persuade her. Later she tells Anna-Maria, Carmel's friend; perhaps she will be able to persuade her to go to hospital. Later I was to see Anna-Maria squatting beside Carmel, rebandaging her swollen leg to make her more comfortable, obviously trying to persuade her to get it attended to properly.

In another part of the station we came across other members of the community handing out food and talking with a group of young Somalians. There was a lot of friendly banter, and then a sudden silence. Policemen were approaching. Moved to one side, we watched as the young Somalians were rounded up and taken away. 'They don't have any permits to be in Italy,' Francesca said. I wondered that she and the others had not intervened at all. 'We will follow it up later,' she said. 'If we protest here, the station authorities will stop us coming.' They have to be discreet as it is. They were not so discreet at Christmas though. That day they had a party at the station; there was champagne to accompany the traditional Christmas meal, and community members and vagrants sat down to feast together as friends. 'I think we must know all the homeless in Rome by name,' Francesca told me as we left the station. She was not boasting, she was just telling me the simple truth.

> The word of the Lord, when assimilated, changes our humanity and opens it to compassion, and demolishes walls of separation and division. Such change in human nature, required of all in the kingdom of God, is closely connected to the dynamism of our faith: the Word of God does not leave us alone, it stops us from being interested only in ourselves and opens us to a desire for a different life. A conversion to God is made manifest by a change in our human lives, in our thought, our

works, our relationships. The liturgy itself would be empty if it did not foster in us a desire to become different, to be renewed, and to renew the world around us. (*Orientations for Our Common Life*)

In twenty years the community has seen some changes take place. There are no longer people living in corrugated iron huts on the outskirts. There are still poor people, but they are not concentrated so much in one place. Poverty has many faces as the community was soon to discover; the old, the infirm, the handicapped, the mentally ill are particularly vulnerable in a city where institutional care can hardly be called care at all. The community were to discover 'outlaw hospitals' that were like 'antechambers of death, where five hundred to a thousand elderly people were hospitalised in conditions that were appalling, but profitable from an economic point of view for those who ran them. Elio discovered Giuseppe in such a place. Giuseppe was an old person living in a hospice which housed three hundred. The place was too large; often he couldn't remember where he was, then he would get angry and scared. The one thing he could remember was the hour each week when Elio came to visit him. Now Elio is one of seven who work full-time at the old people's home run by the community, and Giuseppe lives there, one of fifteen. Elio added, 'Now it is a part of my life to come here every day and wake up Giuseppe. I cannot imagine my life without him.' In addition to the full-time staff, there are twenty-eight volunteers who come to help. It was one of the community's dreams to have such a place. The building was bought with money collected by the community, the city council provides some money to cover running costs, but only enough said Elio to provide 'half breakfast and no lunch'. Some further funding comes from a proportion of the pensions of the elderly people, but without volunteer help the home could not exist. In addition, each old person has particular friends in the community who come to visit them, maybe accompany them on holiday. Some of the old people are also members of the community.

The Community of St Egidio continues to run schools on the outskirts, and in addition to its soup kitchen and residential home for old people, it runs three free nurseries for children and four day-centres for the handicapped. There is also a centre which provides medicine, food and clothing for poor foreigners and refugees from the Third World. Then there are the organised summer holidays for children and teenagers and for the handicapped. These are likely to be the only holidays that some of the community take too. There are free Italian lessons for foreigners and, a recent development, 'The Tent of Abraham', a house provided by the community where refugees can find a temporary home while resettling. Those who stay do so on a self-help basis; the house is divided into four different small communities with some common rooms. Their latest dream is to persuade the city council to let them have the use of a huge abandoned building near to the Piazza di St Egidio. They hope to convert it into a 'citadel of the poor' and to develop many more self-help projects there.

A Way of Life

'WHAT do you do when you just want to relax?' I asked Francesca, when Chris and I went to lunch with her and her friends. She had to think hard before she answered. 'Well, this afternoon I had intended taking Usilia to the hairdressers. Some of the old people are my particular friends; I enjoy going for an outing with one of them. Or going for a walk, eating out, talking with my friends here . . .' Francesca Scambia also has an adopted daughter, Hersio; a three-year-old Somalian girl, who had been found abandoned. She is in a way an adopted daughter to all five women who share the apartment: Francesca Scambia, Francesca Zuccari, Bettina, Claire and Daniela.

Lunchtime is an important part of the daily schedule in the many shared apartments. Then everyone tries to be at home for the meal. After lunch they all scatter to their various jobs in the community. For some, like Francesca Scambia and Daniela these

are their full-time jobs, Francesca responsible for the soup kitchen, Daniela for the work with foreigners and migrants. It is likely to be late when they return in the evening, the custom it seemed to eat supper after evening prayer at St Egidio's – in small groups at a café nearby, or a take-away eaten back at St Egidio's – in the adjacent ex-monastery, which is now the community's offices. Here is where much of the work is administrated, much of it late in the evening.

How did members join? This was difficult to find out. Here no one serves a novitiate, takes vows or makes any formal commitment. There were many people it seemed on the edges, initially drawn by friendship and gradually drawn in by a desire to serve. 'Are you a member?' I asked a young woman sitting in front of me at one of the evening services. 'Oh, I would think I am,' she said. 'Wouldn't you say I am?' she added, asking a friend sitting nearby. The answer was affirmative.

If there is not much distinction made between those who are and who are not members, what is expected of members is clearly understood: prayer, friendship and service of the poor. Not, however, that everyone can give the same amount of time in actual service.

Mario gave as an example some of the women in the communities on the outskirts. 'Some of these women have their work at home, and perhaps they have another job outside too. But if they go to shop in the supermarket and they hear it said that all the old people need to be put in institutions, they have to speak out for a better way. In this way they help to form opinion in their neighbourhood.'

> We all feel the need for total maturity and for renewal; such need develops from the starting point of the person we are, with our own particular background and our own particular history. The rule of love does not drive us towards imitative uniformity, but rather towards a desire to be totally available to the Spirit of the Lord, who brings forth fruit from the richness of diverse humanity, from obedient emulation of the Lord Jesus, whose own humanity is a reference point for all of us in service, in obedience, in humility. (*Orientations for Our Common Life*)

On Sunday Mario drove Chris and me out to visit one of these neighbourhood communities. We attended a Sunday morning service. There were about 150 adults present. During the service hymns were practised that later that week would be sung at a Good Friday service to be held outdoors, and at which it was expected up to three thousand members would be present, from all over Rome and the periphery. Here on the periphery, however, the community had different songbooks to those at St Egidio's; the words were written in large, clear script on sheets clipped into plastic folders, a necessity since some present had reading difficulties and others poor sight. The plight of old people was mentioned again in the sermon. The preacher talked about Jesus being abandoned by many of his friends, and of old people in institutions abandoned by their families and friends. 'Here in these institutions, it is Jesus again who is abandoned. We can go and offer the gift of friendship . . .'

Before the service we met and talked with some of the women. I asked one how she had come to be part of the community. She explained that the community had run a book co-operative in the neighbourhood to help those who could not afford to buy new schoolbooks for their children; old books could be exchanged for new. She had gone along to do this, and had been invited to come back a week later to see some slides. In this way she had met members of the community. 'The friendship I saw was different from anything I'd ever seen before.' Drawn by this, she began to attend a group studying the gospels and came also to see Jesus in a different way. She realised Jesus was concerned about her problems; suddenly he seemed to her 'very close'. Now she spoke of having three jobs: one at home with her family, the second working in the supermarket, the third 'to build a new community here in

Primavalle'. A story very similar to Monica's and others, her words about friendship almost identical to Monica's.

That morning we were told that there were services being held in twenty-five districts on the outskirts; in some districts there might be as many as five separate small communities. The older communities gave support to the newer ones. Members who live in the centre of Rome, visit frequently; they continue to help run the services on the outskirts. We visited a school for children with special needs. The children had worked on a large collage of life in the city of Moscow. 'Yes, here the children's world also gets enlarged,' said Mario. 'They learn about life in Ethiopia, the Sudan, South Africa; the needs of people worldwide.'

It all takes some organising. Each sub-community, each service has its 'responsible person', a kind of team leader. Overall, there is an elected council. This is primarily of lay people; there are priests who sit on it, but the president is always a lay person. Up to this point the president, who is elected for a four-year period, has always been one of the original group of students. We did not meet any of these first visionaries. Mario's wife is one of them, but we did not meet her, or Andrea Riccardi, who was responsible for calling that first meeting. He is now a senior professor at the University of Rome, teaching church history, and still an active member of the community.

It takes money too. Everyone gives what they can, depending on their circumstances. Collections are taken at the services. It took two years to collect enough money to pay for the 'Tent of Abraham'. For the most part, time is given voluntarily, and that helps as do the other forms of sharing that happen. Several times while we were there a member showing us around would run off to see if she or he could borrow so and so's car. After both our lunch stops – the first day at Antonella and Eugenio's, a couple with one child, the second at Francesca's and her friend's – someone arrived to child mind as we all left.

For all the members, the community is a way of life. That it can be for life is important to them, too. Paola, another of our English-speaking guides, mentioned this. She talked about meeting young people from other countries who had spoken to her about their work in some voluntary service at home or overseas and how afterwards they had felt lost, wanting to make a permanent commitment to such a life style, but not knowing how to do this. Paola said she was grateful not to be in the same situation. Recently married, she did not see this as likely to affect her membership.

'Everyone must do everything willingly. That is important,' Mario commented, again talking about permanence of membership. 'If something is not done willingly, the focus will be on yourself, not on Jesus or on the poor, and that in the end will be a problem.'

CHAPTER ELEVEN

Grandchamp

'ARE YOU going to Grandchamp? Would you like a lift?'
The car door opened, and a cheerful face greeted
us. We looked apprehensively at our luggage. 'Come,
come, that's OK,' our newfound friend helped hump the
luggage into the back of his car. 'I know it's only a short walk,
but I think it's worth it.' Exhausted from the long day's train
journey from Rome to Neuchâtel and then on to Areuse, we agreed
gratefully.
As he drove us into the courtyard of the Community of Grandchamp, our friend chatted on. 'I often give people lifts. Well, it is
the least I can do; the sisters are good to me and my family.' And
added as we left, 'Happy Easter'.
It was in fact the Wednesday before Easter. We had arrived in
time for the start of an Easter Retreat.

A Journey

THE Retreat lasted from the Wednesday to the following Monday;
its theme taken from Psalm 31, 'My times are in your hands'.
Although I did not attend all the led meditations, this refrain was
constantly in my mind over the next days as we followed the
sequence of events from Maundy Thursday through to Easter
Sunday.
'You will see how the chapel will be constantly changing over
the next days,' Sister Minke, the 'Responsible Sister', told us.
The main chapel at Grandchamp is the top floor of a large,
converted, wooden barn; below are guest rooms. Inlaid into the
walls of the chapel are pieces of coloured glass, reflecting the light
outside, their many colours and shapes relieving the otherwise dark
sombreness of the barn. At midday the bright colours and shapes
are clearly reflected on the muted shades of the pale carpeted
floor. That first morning, the Thursday in Holy Week, it was
furnished simply as it usually is – a low table which serves
as an altar, two candles, a large wooden cross at one end, a
lectern, two or three icons, benches, prayer stools. It is a place
of simplicity and quiet. Not, however, in winter or even late
spring, a very warm place. There is overhead heating, but then
there are also draughts – a warm jacket or coat is essential –

the sisters mostly wearing their long, warm woollen capes in the chapel. There is another smaller and warmer chapel for private prayer.

That evening the chapel changed for the first time. Tables and chairs were carried from the refectory up the steps into the barn chapel and it became a place to remember together Jesus's last meal with his disciples. Others came from outside to swell our numbers; there was barely room for all two hundred or so, children included. The professed sisters came in their white habits, worn only on feast days and for Sunday Eucharist. We ate the meal in small 'family' groups of ten or twelve – matzet (unleavened bread), lettuce, herbs, cheese, chunks of cold lamb, grape juice to drink. We ate in silence, or more or less – it is difficult to eat matzet in complete silence! Then we moved into the liturgy of the Eucharist – passing the bread and the wine from one to another around the table, still in our family groups.

The meal over, there was a half-hour break, and then back to the chapel for the reading of the farewell discourses from St John's gospel. Parts of the reading were in English and Spanish for the benefit of those of us who did not understand French, Areuse being in the French-speaking part of Switzerland. The tables and chairs had been removed, leaving the chapel almost completely bare, only a few candles left to give a flickering light. The sisters had changed back into their usual blue serge habits. This was a time of preparation for Good Friday, for some the start of a night of prayer, watching with Jesus in the garden of Gethsemane. Some of us stayed only for the service. 'It is important also to get some sleep,' a sister had told us earlier in the day. Tired after three weeks travelling, I slept!

On Good Friday the chapel had been changed again for the liturgy of the Cross. We sat or knelt facing the large wooden cross, at its foot a vase of deep red tulips and a candelabra. The low table had been moved to the centre of the chapel, and again we took Communion, this time standing in a large circle around the table. Many had already observed three hours of silent prayer with Jesus at Golgotha. For some, too, it was a day of fasting. This, however, was not obligatory – for those who wanted it, there was soup and bread and cheese for lunch and again for supper. Breakfast had been as usual – as much bread and jam as you wanted, coffee and tea.

Good Friday ended with prayer around the cross and the Office of the Holy Sepulchre. This time the table was back in its usual position, and in front of it the large wooden Cross had been laid, slightly raised, and on it an icon – a painting of the Cross from the Church of San Damiano, Assisi. At the foot of the Cross, a small bowl of flowers had been placed. The laying of the Cross on the ground symbolised in this service the laying of Christ's body

in the tomb. As one reflective chant or song followed the other, one person after another moved to the foot of the Cross and knelt to pray, sometimes as many as five or six kneeling around the Cross at the same time. At one point a mother brought her young son with her to kneel by the Cross, whispering to him as she did so, no doubt explaining to him the significance of what they were doing. With the scene in the chapel constantly changing in this way, I was aware as never before of how quickly the events we were reliving had followed one on the other, how sudden and quick the change from the intimacy of the Passover meal to Jesus dead and entombed.

Holy Saturday followed. The chapel was as it had been on the Thursday. It was still a day of reflection and prayer, but conversation was less subdued than the previous day. People in twos and threes stopped in the courtyard to chat quietly together, whereas the day before we had passed silently, acknowledging one another but not stopping to talk. At lunchtime Sister Minke encouraged us all to relax during the afternoon, to walk, maybe to rest. She invited us, too, to reflect on the meaning of Easter for us, to consider whether there was anything we wished to leave behind – a personal sin or failing, a hurt or disappointment – whatever might keep us from entering fully into the joy of Easter and its invitation of new life. That, she suggested we wrote down on a piece of paper, and told us to bring the paper to chapel with us at the end of the day.

Pray and work for the coming of the Kingdom.
Throughout your day let work and rest be quickened
    by the Word of God.
Keep inner silence in all things and you will dwell in Christ.
Be filled with the spirit of the beatitudes:
    joy, simplicity, mercy.

This prayer is recited daily by the community during the morning 'colloque' or chapter.

That evening a basin of water had been placed at the foot of the altar, and after joining together in the confession of sins, we were invited to come to the table and place our pieces of paper in the basin, immersing them in the water, symbolising the waters of baptism and new life. Throughout the day I had been thinking how shocked, bereft and lost the friends of Jesus must have been that first Holy Saturday, for at that point they had no hope of Jesus's rising again, and by their observance of the Jewish sabbath were kept even from the act of being able to anoint his dead body. We could anticipate Resurrection, they did not. When I mentioned this to one of the sisters, she replied, 'Yes, but they were together. That is important.'

Saturday ended early at 8.30 p.m., and most of us went to bed,

anticipating an early 5 a.m. start the next morning. Outside each of our rooms the sisters had placed individual vases of spring flowers – the first Easter gifts.

The sisters were up first on Easter morning. Some were possibly up most of the night, for the chapel had been changed again. At 4.30 a.m. we were awakened by the ringing of a bell and a cup of hot tea or tisane. Outside others came from long distances to celebrate the day, up to three hundred of us gathering around the small bonfire the sisters had lit in one corner of the courtyard. At 5 a.m. promptly the sisters came in procession, those professed dressed again in white, Sister Minke carrying the large Easter candle, which, blessed by one of the pastors of the community, was lit from the Easter fire. All of us also had our own small candles, lit, too, from the same fire. 'Le Christ est ressuscité. Alleluia' we sang, as we moved together up the stairs into the barn. 'You see it will be full,' Sister Minke had told Chris earlier in the day. And it was, full with most of us standing, and warm now for once!

This time as we took bread and wine together we celebrated the joy of Easter. 'Christ is risen from the dead, trampling down death by death, and to those in the tomb he has given life.' We sang the refrain again and again, in many languages. As we shared Christ's peace with one another, we greeted each other, 'Christ is risen!'; 'Christ is risen indeed!' came the reply. At first the greetings were hushed, subdued. We were emerging from three days of comparative silence. A voice broke through insistently. It was Sister Minke's encouraging us not to be so reserved. 'Le Christ est ressuscité', she reminded us. Everyone laughed, and began to move and speak more freely and spontaneously. The service over, the greetings continued in the courtyard as friends found each other in the crowd. 'Le Christ est ressuscité.' 'Il est vraiment ressuscité!'

It was now 8.30 a.m. and we sat down to breakfast. This was our first meal not eaten in silence, and there was laughter and conversation. Each table was bright with its vase of Easter flowers; at each place a plate with a hard-boiled egg and several small chocolate eggs in their various coloured wrappings. As usual there were rolls, jam, coffee, tea. Opposite us a young woman picked up her hard-boiled egg and invited the sister sitting next to her to a game of 'crack an egg'. As they banged their eggs together, Chris and I laughed and explained that in England we played a similar game, but with conkers!

This was *not* a day of fasting. We drank wine and ate grapefruit decorated with pieces of kiwi fruit, followed by pork and a dish of assorted vegetables. At this point Sister Minke reminded us to use the bread to clean our plates, for there would be another course. (The custom at Grandchamp is to use only one plate throughout the meal.) 'Non! non!' came the spirited response from her sisters. The third course, generous helpings of vanilla and chocolate ice-cream

with a caramel sauce, was already on individual paper-this-time plates.

'What an enormous amount of work for all of you,' I said to the sister sitting next to me. She nodded in agreement. 'But we shall recover,' she added, laughing.

Not too tired though to sit talking throughout the afternoon to guests and retreatants. The steady hum of conversation, laughter, children playing around the fountain in the courtyard. 'The disciples too had much to talk about after the events of those days, and so have we,' Sister Minke had said to us.

Not too tired either the next day, at the end of the retreat, to join hands and lead us all in a dance, weaving our way in big circles around the courtyard and into lunch, singing *Jubilate Deo*.

Easter had indeed arrived and the weather had changed too. The biting cold wind that had greeted us had changed to warm springlike weather – warm enough to sit out in the small garden, bright with celandine, violets and primroses. Sitting there I thought about the journey we had all taken together. Easter at Grandchamp had helped me to *feel* the events of those days, not only to think about their significance. I had drawn closer to the disciples of Jesus than at any previous Easter, had appreciated in a deeper way what those days must have been like for them; their bewilderment and yet the many ways in which God had drawn alongside and comforted and supported them. I had also come to a firmer resolution about the direction my life was taking. 'My times are in your hands.'

To let the gospel events touch the deepest parts of ourselves where we most need to be affirmed or changed, is at the heart of the contemplative life. 'It is the first time I have felt how deeply Christ suffered,' a young retreatant told me. 'It has touched parts of my own life which I have kept locked away for years.' Then she added, 'I would not have dared to go so deep alone, but here I am with others.'

A Protestant Monasticism

THE Community of Grandchamp evolved like many communities; those responsible did not at first have a community in mind. The buildings had been used as a hospital and in 1931 stood empty. That year a small group of Protestant women, members of the Reformed Church, came to Grandchamp, to spend three days in silence, prayer and meditation. This was a new experience for those who belonged to the Church of the Swiss Reform. Catholics went on retreats; Protestants did not. But these women were determined to find a way to deepen their spiritual life; in 1936 one of the five returned to Grandchamp and opened a house of prayer. One other came to join her; a few years later, a third. Gradually the number

of retreatants grew to the extent that by 1944 these women realised that they had totally underestimated the need for such a house. They also felt their own need for direction and guidance. 'Those women knew nothing of the monastic life, but they were drawn intuitively towards it,' Sister Yvonne told us. 'They began to move towards a discipline of prayer, and when they asked a friend to come and help them, they did not call her leader or chairwoman, but "mother". They were not looking for someone to organise them, but for someone who could help nurture their life in God.' The person whom they approached was Madame Micheli, who in 1931 had been one of the original five. The first monastic profession of the sisters took place in 1952, Madame Micheli (Mother Geneviève) being the first professed. She was then installed as Mother Superior. A Protestant sisterhood had been formed.

A Protestant monasticism was growing not only at Grandchamp, but also in other parts of Europe. The sisters of Grandchamp helped foster it, but they in turn had been influenced by others. Two such influences were a lay movement called Veilleurs (Watchmen), and a movement of liturgical renewal, 'Eglise et Liturgie' (Church and Liturgy). Mother Geneviève and the first sisters had belonged to the Veilleurs before they came to Grandchamp.

The Veilleurs had been founded by a pastor of the French Reformed Church, Wilfred Monod. He had been a chaplain during World War I, and had seen how a disciplined liturgical observance has sustained Catholics and Anglicans, while interned in prison camps. Those who became Veilleurs kept a 'simple rule' which included reciting the Beatitudes each day at noon. This practice is now a part of Grandchamp's midday prayer.

> Blessed are the poor in spirit, for theirs is the kingdom of heaven.
> Blessed are those who mourn, for they will be comforted.
> Blessed are the meek, for they will inherit the earth.
> Blessed are those who hunger and thirst for righteousness, for they will be filled . . .

'They are like our marching orders', a sister said.

Eglise et Liturgie was founded in 1930 by a group of Swiss pastors and lay people. They produced new liturgies for the Church's year and a simple daily office. One of these pastors was Roger Schutz, who later became the founder of Taizé, the Protestant brotherhood in the Burgundian district of France. The 'Office of Taizé' is a development of the Eglise et Liturgie daily office; it is also the prayer book used by the sisters at Grandchamp. There have been and are close links between Taizé and Grandchamp. In 1953 the sisters adopted the rule of Taizé as their own, the rule itself a development of the Veilleurs' 'simple rule' – 'work and pray for the coming of the kingdom'.

There have been other influences; in the early years a number of Anglican communities gave helpful advice and support. These included the Community of St Mary Virgin at Wantage, the Community of the Holy Name, Malvern, and later on the Sisters of the Love of God, Oxford. In more recent years the sisters have also drawn from Eastern Orthodox spirituality. Icons have an important place; the sisters teach others how to use them as aids to prayer and meditation, and a number of sisters paint icons. The manner in which Holy Saturday is observed is inspired by the Orthodox tradition of celebrating the day as the remembrance of the descent of Christ into hell. In this there is an emphasis on prayer for a world where God is often felt to be absent and for people who know what it is to be without hope. In communities like Grandchamp traditions also evolve that are particularly theirs. The rearranging of the chapel furniture to give concrete expression liturgically to the events of Holy Week and of the gospel accounts of the Passion, an example.

> How could we possibly confront the obscenities of today's world, the unleashing of evil, the ravages of sin, without first having contemplated the Holy One? Do you believe that we, men and women of good will, can go down into the hell of sin, violence, doubt, despair and hatred urged on by the simple desire to help one another? The disciples, unable to drive out demons, were certainly men of good will. (Mother Geneviève)

Grandchamp is the mother house, but the sisters also live in many small fraternities in different parts of the world. This development began when a Lutheran congregation asked the community if one or two sisters could come and live among them to help the pastor in his work. Similar requests followed. There are now fraternities in other parts of Switzerland, also in France, Algiers and Israel.

Each fraternity is set up to meet a particular need and all are in places of real need. They are 'a sign of the love of Christ in the midst of social misery'. The small group of sisters – two or three – that make up each fraternity keep the same rule as those at Grandchamp and the same pattern of daily prayer. There is, however, necessarily a flexibility and simplicity to the way they pray together, the need to adapt, to be open to change. It was here in one of the small fraternities that rearranging the chapel furniture during Holy Week was first tried, and gradually afterwards introduced at Grandchamp.

I talked with Sister Maria who is one of three sisters who form a *fraternity* close to a psychiatric clinic near Lausanne in Switzerland. They had been asked to come to be with the patients in the clinic; 'to share in their life, to integrate it into our own life and to bring it in prayer to God'. It is one of those places, said Maria, where the Church often does not know how to enter in, or how to speak

about faith and hope and death and resurrection. For Maria it is an important place to be, and where she is made constantly aware of how particular groups of people are vulnerable in today's society, '... those who are very aware, artists for instance, and young people, who turn to drugs, alcohol or suicide because our world is too hard and because of the whole danger to life itself with the bomb and much else.' Exactly the same problems, she said, that many of the young people who came to Grandchamp on retreat or as helpers spoke about.

A Red Thread . . .

THERE is a rhythm to life at Grandchamp. Each day starts not in the morning but in a time of preparation the night before. It is a practice that has its roots in Jewish spirituality; the Jewish sabbath begins the preceding evening, on the Friday. The last act of each day for a sister is to read the gospel for the following day. The night is seen as a time of abandonment to God, an entering into the darkness with him, a time when the words of the gospel are able to touch the deepest unconscious and transform it.

Morning begins at 5.30 a.m. in solitude before God, During this time of personal prayer each sister reads the same gospel passage again and meditates on it. Breakfast is self-service and silent and followed by thirty minutes of spiritual reading – reading from a book on the contemplative life. At 7.45 a.m. the sisters join the guests for morning prayer in the big barn (called 'the Ark') or in the smaller chapel, if numbers are few. Again, the same gospel passage is read and there is prayer about the needs of that day.

Immediately Morning Prayer is over the sisters gather in their community room. They form a large circle, and a passage is read from the Rule of Taizé. This is a time when the sisters share small things they are thankful for, and also say sorry for anything they have done amiss. '. . . only those things that touch the common life, that hurt the whole. It is all very simple', said Sister Vreni. A sister may ask for prayer for some need. Details of the day are gone over: who is leaving, who is arriving, what needs to be done.

> Then the greatest miracle, and the most natural, takes place. From our poor lives and our poor hearts the life of Christ shines forth. We bear it within us and those whom we meet greet Christ in us. Then everything is adoration, love, silence. There is no striving to imitate Christ. Christ prays in us. Christ lives in us. We shall never achieve a life of prayer on our own strength. But we can open up our heart to Christ, receive him, and with him be nothing but prayer. (Mother Geneviève)

What needs to be done – the daily work – includes work in the kitchen, the laundry, the garden and also the welcoming of guests. The welcome at Grandchamp is always personal. There is always one sister who is there to welcome you, to listen to you, to give direction if you are there on retreat. She will notice if you are not at a meal, and come to see if you are all right. A vase of flowers and a small welcome note will greet you on arrival. Work as well as prayer is part of the rhythm of each day. '. . . prayer is like a red thread that runs through and holds all together'. 'It is very strong to be held together like that,' said Vreni.

Midday prayer is at 12 noon. This is the time when the Beatitudes or part of them are read or maybe sung. Again all or part of the same gospel passage will be read. '. . . in the morning you may have been so busy that you have forgotten by midday what you read earlier; it is a reminder . . .'

Meals are also an important part of the daily rhythm. They are simple. A meal may consist of lettuce with a mayonnaise dressing, followed by a rice and vegetable risotto. Care is given to how each meal is served and to each other's needs at table. Again there are the personal touches. Each guest has her or his own serviette, the name pinned to it. There are always freshly arranged flowers on each table. Part of the meal is eaten in silence, part is for conversation. All the sisters join with the guests for the midday meal; at the evening

meal usually only one group of sisters is present. 'Each meal should be an agapé [a love feast], and should express something of God's goodness', Vreni told us. '. . . in many homes today meals are often eaten in front of the television, or rushed'. There is no rush at Grandchamp, and even the silence is friendly. At lunch, too, one sister will summarise the headlines of that day's world news.

After lunch the sisters maintain silence until 3 p.m. This is time they can use for resting or walking or writing letters. They will also take thirty minutes for personal prayer during the afternoon if it can be fitted in with work. Evening Prayer is at 6.30 p.m., before the evening meal. The epistle – a reading from one of the letters in the New Testament – is read. This is also when time is spent in interceding for the needs of the world. The prayers are amazingly informed. 'How do you know so much about events all over the world?' I asked Vreni. 'You can't have much time for watching television or reading magazines or papers.' Her answer was revealing. 'It comes from people we know. They write and tell us their stories, what is happening, what their needs are.' People do come from all over the world. 'Sometimes I look around the table at midday and wonder at it,' said Vreni. 'There is a young man from Corrymeela in Northern Ireland, and across the table from him a man from Eastern Germany. Always there are so many different parts of the world represented just in that one small gathering.'

The sisters eat the evening meal in their small family groups of seven to nine sisters. After that there may be a short meeting, a time of sharing or a meeting of the professed sisters. Then comes Compline and again the entrance into the night as preparation for the next day.

As each day has its rhythm so does each week. For the sisters at Grandchamp the Easter message of resurrection life is at the heart of their corporate life. Each week – starting on the Saturday evening – begins with a reading from the Easter story, or a passage from the epistles about the Resurrection of Jesus. 'Easter is our point of reference; the starting place for each week, each new day.' Monday is what the sisters call their 'desert day' – during the morning strict silence is observed, this is time for prayer; during the afternoon there is a community meeting. The meeting begins with prayer for the community's needs, and continues with all the many decisions that have to be made week by week. Some of the larger decisions will be taken at meetings of the fully professed sisters. A small group 'around Sister Minke' helps to prepare for these meetings, and keeps a caring eye on the community's needs and administration.

Potential For Life

A COMMUNITY of prayer, that which Christ calls the Church to be – and the Church exists wherever two or three are gathered in his name – is a place where the glory of God is manifested in the potential for life, where we contemplate the fullness of his revelation', Mother Geneviève wrote of the contemplative life. It is a spirituality that sees the Christian vocation as a gradual process by which each person is transformed into the image of God that she or he carries within. A desire to realise this potential has drawn many to Grandchamp, and the call to join the community has taken a number by surprise.

Sister Maatje came as a student, seeking 'a faith she had lost'. She had no intention of becoming a sister, but was intrigued by what she found. 'All these women together, there must be something to it.' Uncomfortably she began to feel that maybe God was calling her to the same life. To put the uncomfortable feeling to rest, she decided to spend two months at Grandchamp 'to get it out of my system'. She is now one of the professed sisters and laughs as she remembers her initial discomfort. But others had similar experiences. Sister Helen felt that God might be calling her to become a missionary, and came to Grandchamp as a time of preparation. While there, she began to feel that God wanted her to pursue this calling as a sister of Grandchamp. She was shocked, she told me. To think the matter over she went to Lee Abbey for eight months, and afterwards returned to Grandchamp as a postulant. That was almost thirty years ago.

Those who come to join the community spend their first year as postulants, and then a period of time as novices. The length of the novitiate is different for each sister. There has to be adequate time for inner healing. 'Today people have more and more deep hurts', Vreni, who is assistant novice mistress, explained. '. . . perhaps it is because they carry such deep hurts that they are looking for God, or for meaning in life'. Healing comes as these often buried hurts are faced. It is only after there has been enough time for this 'inner work' that it is possible to enter fully into the life of the community, Vreni said. In their last two or three years novices are introduced gradually into the gatherings of the professed sisters. By this time a sister will have 'learnt how to cope with her inner life at a more adult level'. It is all a process of growing up, of becoming that unique 'personality in Christ', of realising your potential for life.

It is the way 'to become more human, more compassionate, more gentle towards others as Christ was. To enter into ourselves and discover God is there, so very close to us, is this not the secret of the radiant life?' Mother Geneviève wrote.

Easter 1989 was my second visit to Grandchamp. The first had been at a time of personal crisis. I had gone wanting to know how to deepen my own life of prayer. I left realising that to pursue this path would mean a total reordering of my whole way of life. It is places like Grandchamp that help show others of us the way.

To be a parable of community calls for living the process of death and resurrection daily. Many of our sisters are fragile and have been scarred by the war and the disintegration of family life and indeed of European civilization itself. A long healing process is necessary in order for our sisters to become totally available to God's Word working through them. The work of reconciliation is essentially a work of forgiveness. Forgiveness is the center of our life together. (Sister Minke)

Chapter Twelve

Post Green

'HERE is where we plan to build the recreation and therapy centre for the disabled. It will include a swimming-pool, games room and a therapy room. These marks here are places where the log-cabins will be; each cabin will accommodate about six or eight people.'

Jodi Page-Clark had the large plan spread out on the table in the dining-room at Sparrow's Nest, the farmhouse at East Holton. I had driven over with Chris to introduce him to Jodi and to the Page-Clark family. We were soon all bending over the plans and envisaging the future East Holton Centre.

'Here close to the pine woods,' Jodi continued, 'is where the pastoral centre will be, here on the edge of the wood. We thought . . .' Jodi continued explaining the various parts of the plan to Chris. I remembered the first time that I had come with Faith Lees to see the farmhouse at East Holton and to walk down through the pine woods to the shoreline and to look across the waters of Poole Harbour to the distant Purbeck Hills. We had plans that time, too; to use East Holton as the site for Post Green's summer camps. I was excited at the possibility: as a camp site it was ideal. It has proved to be over these past seventeen years. Now the community is planning further development.

Chris had come down from London to visit the Post Green Community. This time I did not have to leave home. A member of the community until 1985, I still live close by. It was Chris who asked most of the questions this time.

'What do you do as a community?' was one question. Jodi explained that the community was a caring and teaching community. Then added, 'It is not the things we do that make the community what it is, but the way in which we do them. The things we do as a community can change, but not how we go about them.'

Change is nothing new for the Post Green Community. It has experienced many changes in its fifteen years.

City of Refuge

MAY 3rd, 1975, is Post Green's official birthday. On that day the Bishop of Salisbury presided over a Service of Commitment in Lytchett Minster parish church. Forty-two people made an act of commitment.

The beginnings of the community, however, go much further back. Post Green is the name of a house, the home of (Sir) Tom and (Lady) Faith Lees. When telling their story, Tom and Faith always recall that Madeline Lees, Tom's mother, prayed constantly for the house 'to be used for the glory of God'. Tom brought up in such a Christian home says he cannot remember a day when Jesus was not his best friend.

Madeline Lees was an ardent Christian, and a ceaseless organiser. She turned the village of Lytchett Minster into a mini-Oberammergau, and with the villagers as the cast made two religious films, one of the life of John the Baptist, the other about the life of Jesus, using Handel's *Messiah* as its background theme. In the early years of her marriage, Faith Lees was drawn into her mother-in-law's many activities. With a young family to bring up, the strain told on her, and resulted in a nervous breakdown. While she was recovering, Faith and Tom went to Lee Abbey for a holiday, and it was while she was at Lee Abbey that Faith came to believe that God could help her. She prayed the first real prayer of her life. 'God, if you can do anything for me, come into my life, and cope please. Because I can't manage by myself.'

Faith's mother, Muriel Jessiman, was also a deeply religious woman, a member of the Oxford Group (a movement that emphasised listening prayerfully to God to receive practical and concrete guidance for action) and a woman of prayer. Faith now began to read some of her mother's books on prayer, and found herself drawn particularly to the writings of a Spanish saint, Teresa of Avila. She and Tom began to throw themselves with enthusiasm into the life of the local church, an enthusiasm that was not always appreciated or, it seemed, wanted. 'Is this all the Church has to offer or to give?' they would often grumble. 'No,' a friend told them when he came to supper one evening; there was more. Reg East, an Anglican clergyman, had come into a new experience of the work of the Holy Spirit in his life. That evening he prayed for Tom and Faith to be filled with the Holy Spirit.

This was to be a major turning-point in Tom and Faith's life. It was to lead within five years to Post Green's becoming a centre for a teaching and healing ministry as part of the rapidly growing charismatic movement, with its emphasis on a renewal of the gifts of the Holy Spirit: healing, prophecy and speaking in tongues included. The paddock at the back of the Post Green house became a site for large summer camps, the house itself was turned into a mini-conference centre, two hundred or more crammed into the hallway and the two rooms either side of it. People came seeking healing, both physical and emotional. There were some startling answers to prayers for healing. On one occasion a woman who came in a wheelchair walked away healed. She had been crippled by arthritis and also had a weak heart. She has not needed the wheelchair since that day.

Some of those who came seeking emotional healing were to take longer to recover. A few Tom and Faith drew into their family as short-term guests to aid their growth and recovery. Faith in her reading of the lives of the saints and in particular the life of Teresa of Avila had come to realise that it is an experience of the love of God that brings lasting healing. And those who came to Post Green, whether for just a day or for longer, found themselves touched in an unusual way by the knowledge that they were loved.

The cost, however, to the Lees family was considerable. It was obvious to many who came to the conferences that Tom and Faith needed help in the growing work. A team of helpers began to form. Some came from local churches; others from farther afield moved to Lytchett Minster or nearby to be part of this team. I came from London to help for a few months and that was almost twenty years ago!

> [Today God] is stirring up in the hearts of mankind, young and old, rich and poor, an overpowering desire to find the truth. He is taking us back to himself, to his integrity and reality, to a quality of knowledge which allows for no compromise . . . He

is forcing us to come to terms with his breadth and length and height and depth through the love which he is pouring into our hearts which are crying out for hope and understanding. He is calling people to contemplate him, to discover him in the stillness of their minds and hearts, to know his mystical love. He wants us to climb out of our boxes, break down our barriers, dive below the surface and find in ourselves a new nature, that of God himself. (Faith Lees, *Break Open My World*)

At that point we did not think in terms of anything very permanent. Post Green was meeting a need at a particular point in time. It was a place where those who had come into a new experience of the work of the Holy Spirit in their lives could find support and teaching. Those who came included numbers of ordained men and women, of all denominations. It was Faith who first began to feel that God wanted something more permanent. One day when she was praying, the name Ramoth-Gilead popped into her mind. She did not know of any place with that name, but the words went round and round in her mind. It was Tom who told her that Ramoth-Gilead was the name of a city mentioned in the Old Testament, the first of ten cities of refuge. Faith had been praying about Post Green, seeking some clearer understanding of what God was doing. Now she began to feel that what God wanted was a modern-day *city of*

refuge. 'Not just one home, but many homes: a place where people could come and find rest and refreshment, healing.'

In 1973 Tom, Faith and I visited a number of places in the United States that, like Post Green, had become centres for teaching as part of the charismatic renewal. We thought we might get some further insights from our visit. What emerged was the idea of Post Green as a community.

Outcome of Change

W E LITTLE knew what a tangle becoming a community would eventually get us into. There were to be many ups and downs. This led us to seek advice, and we turned to an American Episcopalian minister, the Rev. Graham Pulkingham, who at the invitation of the (then) Bishop of Coventry had come to England to share his experience of living in community with the Church in England. While here in England Graham founded the Community of Celebration with its home first near Reading in Berkshire, and later for a period on the island of Cumbrae, off the Scottish coast. There are now two Communities of Celebration, one here in England in Bletchingley, Surrey, and one in America near Pittsburgh. For a number of years Post Green became a Community of Celebration,

joining the caring and teaching aspects of Post Green's ministry with the outreach ministry of the Community of Celebration, notably that of the Fisherfolk travelling teams that demonstrated and taught the use of folk arts in worship. The community grew larger, at one time numbering around seventy or more members. This included children. We lived in extended family households, each household drawing a living allowance from the community's 'common pot', and settled down to live that way for the rest of our lives – or so we thought.

It was a severe shock when the recession that hit the country in the late 1970s hit us too. Part of our 'common pot' income came from the sale of Fisherfolk records, cassettes and songbooks, part from people's gifts and from our camps and conferences, and part from a number of businesses we ran – a small publishing house, a commercial caravan site, a village shop and a petrol station. All these were affected by the recession. Our situation was complicated, too, by the fact that for the most part the community lived in houses on the Lees estate, and Tom was still in the process of transferring a part of his estate to the 'common pot', legally a lengthy business. During this time of financial crisis a number left the community, and a decision was reached to separate the two ministries, that of Post Green and of the Community of Celebration. It was a painful time and a difficult decision.

Post Green is much smaller now; fifteen adults and six children. Five of these members met with Chris and myself and talked about the changes that have taken place since that time, and some of the positive outcomes.

One of the first outcomes of not being able to sustain a 'common pot' was the realisation that if Post Green's healing and caring ministry was to be sustained then it needed to be put on a more professional basis and fees charged for counselling. The community had already established a close relationship with a Christian psychiatrist, Frank Lake, founder of clinical theology. Frank Lake died in 1982, but by that time several members of Post Green had already attended training sessions at his centre in Nottingham. Following this, several members also received training in spiritual direction, and in 1984 a pastoral centre was opened offering counselling, therapy, short-term residential care and also spiritual direction and retreats. A former colleague of Frank Lake's, Brian Hawker, was asked to become supervisor to the centre, and its staff also began to work closely with local doctors and psychiatrists. Two of the community, Carolyn Reinhart and Gerry O'Meara, have been consistently its full-time staff with others available part-time.

The work of the pastoral centre is seen as an extension of the long-standing healing and caring ministry of the community. Its emphasis is on the integration and healing of the whole person. Those coming for short-term residential care live as part of the family, as in the early days. Post Green house is the present home of the pastoral centre, and all six community members who live there make up the team that support its residential care and retreat work. Seminars and courses on prayer and on healing and growth are also held there from time to time.

The increased professionalism has not changed the essence of what those seeking counselling or direction find at Post Green. '... a consistent love over years, often painful – just insistent enough to keep me from withdrawing, gentle enough for me to trust'. It is the knowledge that they are loved that continues to be central to people's experience.

Another outcome of the changes that took place between 1984 and 1986 was 'to push the community out into the area more'. A number of members now have full- or part-time jobs that bring them daily into contact with people locally. David Palmer manages the South Lytchett caravan site, Linda Palmer runs a nursery school, Ruth and Arthur Vincent the village post-office and stores, Chris Kelleway is a self-employed gardener, Margaret Mather works part-time for the diocese, and part-time for a local charity, Daphne Mills is a colour consultant and Annie Forshaw works one night a week at an old people's nursing home. In addition to these jobs, community members are active in both the local Anglican and Catholic churches.

A former community household has become a conference and arts centre, run not by members of the community but with the same caring ethos as Post Green. Jodi and Howard Page-Clark at Sparrow's Nest have an adopted family of four and also a ministry to young adults, who are in need of support and vocational guidance and who come as short-term residents and live as members of the family. Rachael Rutter uses her home to accommodate guests who come to visit the community. Others in the neighbourhood who are close friends of the community take as lodgers some of those who have been short-term residents and want a transitional period nearby before making a permanent move.

'It's as though the vision we had of city of refuge is taking shape and we've hardly noticed it happening,' said Faith Lees. The development of the East Holton centre is also a part of this same vision.

Poole Harbour is Britain's largest harbour, its hinterland one of the most important conservation areas in Britain. The Dorset heathland is unique, its soil nurturing rare mosses and heather. The plan that the community has for the development of the area of heathland around East Holton combines a number of dreams that the community has about its future activities: a centre for the disabled, a place for environmental studies and a more permanent retreat centre.

The large camping field with its nearby shower block and small self-catering kitchen already has facilities for the disabled. As a camp site it is used each year by the community for its own camps, and increasingly also by other organisations – local Spastic Society schools, and Cubs and Scouting groups. Future facilities will include a recreation/therapy centre designed primarily for use by disabled people and their families, a large kitchen/dining facility with TV lounge, laundry and showers, a number of small log cabins, winterised for year-round use, and a building for environmental studies which will be subdivided into classrooms, a craft room and a laboratory. The facilities will be available not only for the disabled, but they will have priority. Other groups that the community hope will use the centre are families under stress, including families of AIDS sufferers and those who live with and look after the chronically disturbed.

The retreat centre with its own reception block and cabins is to be developed far enough away from the other facilities to make it a quiet place for those who come on retreat. The two developments, however, are linked, the retreat centre also seen as a place where those under stress can find counselling and spiritual direction or just a place to recoup and rest.

Another part of the plan is to offer a year's training programme to young adults where they can help to care for and work alongside disabled young people, learn themselves about the needs of the environment and also take time to pray and think about the direction of their own lives. The latter is a natural development of the kind of support that Jodi and Howard already give to the young adults who come to stay in their home.

It will take a while before the plan is fully implemented, but since it is a development of what already exists, its growth can take place in stages. The community is already in contact with various organisations for the disabled, and a number have promised support in fund-raising and promotion. The dream is not so far off, though; David Fieldsend, who spent a year in the community after school and before university, has just returned having completed a degree in environmental studies. He has joined the Sparrow's Nest household, and will help with the laying of nature trails and with the setting-up of the centre for environmental studies.

Cost of Commitment

POST Green is an ecumenical community. It is open to Christians of all denominations; at present it has both Anglican and Roman Catholic members. On the first Monday of every month the community has an open evening with an invited speaker. There are a number of other occasions when the community is joined by friends who live close by. Once a month there is an evening meeting for prayer and worship, and on Wednesdays at 6.30 a.m. each week a prayer-meeting, with an emphasis on praying for the needs of the neighbourhood. Every Thursday at 5.40 p.m. there is a simple agapé (love feast). The agapé is a short service of songs, prayers and readings with plenty of time for sharing news and requests for prayer. There is also a short talk, or more usually a drama or mime with the children taking part. It ends with the sharing of bread and wine, and is followed by a pot-luck supper. The evening Chris joined us the pot-luck included cake and champagne! Tom and Faith were celebrating their fortieth wedding anniversary.

Members of the community meet together at other times, too. Three times a week there is a short service at the end of the work day at either Post Green or Sparrow's Nest. Residents and guests also attend. Twice a month on Monday evenings the community gathers for a business meeting.

Administrating the community is simpler now than in the past, since numbers are fewer. There is no leader or director; Howard Page-Clarke is the community administrator. All major decisions are taken by the community as a whole at its business meetings. One sub-group, the family life group, is responsible for the pastoral health of the community. Another, the membership group, interviews and makes recommendations about prospective new members.

Potential members first spend a period in one of the community's households. The next step with the agreement of the whole community is to become a novice. That is for at least a two-year period, includes spending three months living as part of a community household, and concludes with a one- to three-week retreat. The retreat is a time of weighing-up the cost and considering whether God's call is truly to Post Green. 'The real cost is being open to change in your own life,' Faith Lees explained. 'People ask to join the community from a desire to help others, and then discover it's a matter of becoming vulnerable yourself. They may expect that, but usually don't expect it to be so painful.' The whole community is again involved in agreeing to a person's becoming a full member, and after that membership is renewed annually. Most consider their membership to be permanent.

The community's rule of life was the result of six months' careful deliberation by the present members of the community two years ago. It returns to Faith's original vision of the community and its surrounds as a place of refuge. It states that there is only one real refuge and that is God, but that God's people are also called to build together an environment where God's love is felt not just taught, a place where those in need can find refuge and be strengthened. In order to build that environment, community members commit themselves to learn how to love, to develop disciplines of prayer and personal growth, to take part in the corporate worship of the community and also of a local church, to use their homes as places of hospitality and of healing for others, and to be willing to share their possessions

---

Rule of Life (shortened)

The City of Refuge
Psalm 36:7–9
How precious is thy steadfast love, O God!
   The children of men take refuge in the shadow of thy wings.
They feast on the abundance of thy house,
and thou givest them drink from the rivers of thy delight.
For with thee is the fountain of life;
in thy light do we see light.

The City of Refuge is a place where God's people live out a life dependent on God's mercy. As we know his mercy and refuge, so we can share this knowledge with others.

The Rule of Love
Our commitment to love each other is a commitment to 'walk in the light', which means being prepared to keep our relationships open, honest, gentle and vulnerable.

Prayer and Worship
We are committed to the discovery of a continually deepening relationship with God. This happens through a disciplined personal prayer life and committed corporate worship life. As we are an ecumenical Community we need to have an openness to change, to broaden our outlooks and to share different understandings.

Hospitality
The quality of love and faith in our homes is the foundation of the healing ministry. We are committed to an open sharing of our homes.

The Sharing of Possessions
Each member of the Community is a steward before God of their possessions and responsible to God in relationship to their money and their giving. Any giving must come from the fullness of the heart, from the abundance found in God's refuge and in thankfulness for his abundant mercy to them.

Obedience and Service
We are committed to obedience to the Rule of Life and willing service to each other.

in a spirit of openness to the needs of others. The latter is a change from the time when as a community our needs were met from the one common purse. For Faith Lees it is the harder discipline. 'Somehow the common purse cloaked the reality of the situation that some had more money and security than others. Now we are having to discover what sharing means in a more real way.'

It all comes back to Jodi's comment, 'It is not the things we do that makes the community what it is, but the way in which we do them.' Learning to be consistent in loving and caring is what membership is about; a consistency to be worked out in all the daily tasks of gardening or managing a caravan site or selling stamps in the post-office. *Learning* is the key word. 'It doesn't mean we've arrived,' Gerry O'Meara told a gathering of Post Green camp helpers at a planning day, 'it means admitting our failures and yet remaining open to God's grace and to his power to change and heal us.'

Each member undertakes to review her or his life with the help of a spiritual director, as part of the annual review. The community itself has a visiting consultant who is on hand to give objective advice and supervision, at present, Brian Hawker.

Camp Programme

ONE Post Green tradition that has stayed untouched by all the changes that have taken place are the camps that happen each spring bank-holiday. The camp is divided into a number of 'family units', each unit with its small team of camp helpers. The aim is to draw those who come into a loving and caring extended family life. The 'family', however, has reshaped itself over the years. Previously it was the community itself that primarily provided this sense of family; now it is the wider network of Post Green friends who run the camps, together with members of the community. Many of these friends have attended Post Green camps as campers or helpers for many years. Some came first as teenagers. A special feature of the camps over the years has been separate programmes for children and young people run alongside the adults' programme, almost three camps in one.

In recent years the summer camps have been a place for exploring the wider issues of healing and reconciliation in society. Through its counselling work the community is made constantly aware of the pressures in today's society that cause stress and breakdown. Increasingly it is young men and women in their twenties or early thirties who come seeking therapy and counselling, some as short-term residents. 'The structures of present-day society do not give these young people a firm foundation for building life,' said Faith Lees. Many had questions about the purpose of life itself, questioning the sense of pursuing a career or marrying and having a family when the world itself was endangered by the bomb and pollution.

A Christian's responsibility for society, to change situations of injustice and to help build community, have been the themes of past camps. The weekend Chris came to visit, camp helpers were preparing for the 1989 camp, its theme reconciliation. One of the speakers was Elias Chacour, a Melkite priest, who as a Palestinian living on the West Bank works to bring about reconciliation between Arabs and Jews. Another speaker was John Sentamu, a black Anglican priest, who shared about his experiences of working for reconciliation in the multiracial, multicultural setting of Britain's cities.

Those who attend the camps come from many different parts of Britain, as many as three hundred in one camp. Morning discussion groups at camp are a lively interchange of how to work out in many different situations the challenge to become an active force for peace and reconciliation in society. At home, members of Post Green community pursue this in a number of different ways. Carolyn and Gerry are part of a justice and peace group at their Roman Catholic church, Ruth and Arthur sell Traidcraft products, Chris has a particular concern for the environment and for recycling waste, a number support different developmental projects. Last year Post Green household spent the best part of Christmas Day helping to serve meals at a soup kitchen in Bournemouth. The development of the East Holton centre has grown out of a corporate concern for the environment and also out of a desire to share a place of rural beauty with others who may have little or no opportunity to enjoy the countryside, in particular, the disabled and those who live under stress in inner-city areas.

The community also has close links with a community of reconciliation in South Africa, the Broken Wall Community, founded in 1985 by Graham and Dorcas Cyster. The vision for this non-racial life-style community came during a six-year period that Graham spent at Post Green following a crisis of faith in his own life. He is a Baptist minister, so-called 'coloured' from the Cape, Dorcas, an American Mennonite.

The Test

POST Green's extended family is worldwide. Tom and Faith had just returned from a three months' trip to Australia, New Zealand and North America, and so news of the extended family was still being shared with others during the time that Chris visited the community. Tom told a group of us how much it had meant to visit families who were still putting into practice

what they had learnt at Post Green, and who still felt so much like a part of Post Green's family. There were three families in particular that they visited; all three had been a part of the community for a number of years.

Some years back we made a film about the community, *For Our Life Together*. In it Howard Page-Clarke made a comment that has stuck in all our minds. 'I think,' he said, 'that what community is about is the quality of our relationships. That's the test and that is what will last.'

O my Lord, what a great comfort
it is to me that Thou didst not entrust
the fulfilment of Thy will
to one so wretched as I!
Blessed be Thou for ever and
let all things praise Thee.
May Thy name be for ever glorified.
I should indeed have had to be good,
Lord, if the fulfilment or non-fulfilment
of Thy will (in Heaven and on earth)
were in my hands.
But as it is, though my will is not
yet free of self-interest,
I give it to Thee freely.
For I have proved, by long experience,
how much I gain by
leaving it freely in Thy hands.
 Teresa of Avila, *The Way of Perfection*

A favourite prayer of Faith Lees